Decomposing
The Shadow

Lessons From The
Psilocybin Mushroom

James W. Jesso

Decomposing The Shadow

Lessons From The Psilocybin Mushroom

SOULSLANTERN

SoulsLantern Publishing
Calgary, Canada

Disclaimer:

This book is intended as an informational guide for educational and philosophical purposes. Neither the author nor the publisher encourage, endorse, or support illegal or dangerous behavior of any kind. Readers assume full responsibility for their choices and actions, including but not limited to, any physical, psychological, or social consequences resulting from the ingestion of psychedelic substances or their derivatives.

Cover Design: Phillip Vernon of Third Eye Arts
Inner layout: Melanie Goodfellow
Editing: Marty Grant & Jasmine Leah Griffeth
Publication graciously crowdfunded by community supporters

978-0-9919435-0-0
ISBN

CONTENTS

- Getting There Without Drugs
- Dagobah as a Proverb for the Psychedelic Journey
- Psychosocial Evolution

"What we are talking about is something of immense importance because unless there is a fundamental revolution in each one of us, I do not see how we can bring about a vast, radical change in the world. And surely, that radical change is essential."

-J. Krishnamutri
As One Is:
To Free The Mind from All Conditioning

Acknowledgements

This book is the largest project I have seen to completion at this point in life. By and far, the only reason it made it to this point is through the help and support of an entire community of people, some of which I have never met and never will. It would be a book in itself to mention all the people who helped inspire me to take a leap on this creative project. What follows is a partial list.

Throughout the course of my development as a conscious being, there have been several authors and teachers who inspired me with their ideas and actions. Those who were most influential in developing the supportive ideas to this book include Jiddu Krishnamurti, Baba Ram Dass, Chögyam Trungpa, Terrence McKenna, Neal Goldsmith, and Martin W. Ball. The manner in which these people presented their conceptual frameworks for the nature of mind, reality, experience, and personal growth unlocked whole new realms of experience and investigation in my life. Without these realms, this book wouldn't have happened.

The development of this book had few hands directly molding it, but those that did played a major role. In no particular order, I extend gratitude to Marty Grant for the many hours he spent with the manuscript and with me, tearing it down so we could rebuild it better than before. It was with him that I really began to grasp the breadth of this work. A similar thank you goes to Jasmine Griffeth who also spent hours with the manuscript ensuring it was readable, constant, and followed grammatical rules as often as possible. Tyler Hayden, author of Ohmhole, was the first trained eye to see my manuscript and set the stage for its journey towards publication. It was from his initial involvement that he offered "Decomposing The Shadow" as the title of this book, which has resonated on multiple levels through its development since then. His encouragement to take the manuscript to publication played a big part in the sense of worth I had regarding this project. I'd also like to thank Melanie Goodfellow for designing the innards of this book and the SoulsLantern Publishing logo. Also, big thanks to Phi Vernon of Third Eye Arts for the amazing cover (and all the other design work he has done for me).

In the last stages of this book's development, I began a crowd-funding campaign through Indigogo. In doing so, a community that spanned from my font door and family to all across the globe, gave me a chance and showed me they believed in my project. Without that support, this project would not have made it.   With the campaign, there are two people I would like to personally thank. The first is Jared Smith, a man I met through the politically conscious community of Calgary and went above and beyond in donating a huge amount of funds to my project. The second is Maximillian Krewiak, who made all the videos for the campaign on the exchange of dinner and being taught how to make raw chocolate from scratch. Without his amazing camera skills, I am certain the campaign would not have made its goal.

Writing and publishing a book is by no means a venture with a low price tag. I am infinitely grateful for the support of paying in barter and being offered a "mate's rate" from so many people.

The last group of people I would like to thank hits close to home (literality). The conversations I shared with fellow researchers and explorers Andriy Anatolyevich, Travis Cartwright, Andrew Daniels, and Matt Koczkur about the broader implications of the psychedelic experience was a great help in the development of these ideas. Kyle Flemmer, a friend and brother of long, was the first person with the confidence and compassion to explicitly show me where my writing sucked and offered me invaluable tools to becoming better at it. Clea Schmidt, a great friend from Australia, was the first person to not only believe in my ability to succeed at grand dreams, but to invest herself into supporting me even when I had nothing but hope.

Joshua Curtis John Walker, an artist whose skill and visions awakened the artist in me when we were teenagers, came with me as my sober sitter on my first two intentional psilocybin ceremonies. He was really there for me during my early experimentation with mushrooms as a tool for healing; even when I was going out on my own to journey, I could show up at his house in the middle of the night and he would sit with me and listen if I need someone to talk to. Since we were teenagers he has been a friend in whom I have shared some of the deepest, strangest, most enlightening conversations about life, love, and everything. His friendship is something I hold very dear.

The bulk of this book was originally written in my wonderful friend Sara Kasserman's loft apartment in front of a massive bay window overlooking the city. I have infinite thanks for her giving me a key to come and drink obscene amount of yerba mate at her desk while she was at work. Sara has been and ongoing presence of support and love in my life since I moved to Calgary. She was the first person since moving back out west that offered me a sense of 'home away from home', to which I am deeply grateful.

When moving to Calgary, Alberta I got involved with a group called Evolver Calgary. As a part of this group I was offered not only a recognition of my value, but the support of having a space to offer it openly through public presentations and event coordination. During my time with Evolver, Matt 'Skye Dreamer' Catley, Joshua Wagler, and Kym Chi have been personal role models and an invaluable source of inspiration.

Lastly, I want to thank my parents and my sister. They have been there my entire life as beacons of love and support. My sister, Jessica, has shown her belief in me through massive amounts of support in all my projects. I couldn't of asked to have such a wonderful woman as my little sister. My parents, James and Angela, gave almost everything to nourish and care for my sister and I. Without the ongoing recognition, love, affection, support, and openness they have showed me throughout my entire life, I would be nothing. In regards to this project, they have supported me every step of the way, even though its premise directly confronted their views on drugs and spirituality. I feel blessed and honored to have such great family.

To everyone whose name was not here, but who continues to support me, thank you.

PRELUDE

Humankind is of the Earth, and the integrity of our physiological and psychological systems rely on maintaining constructive relationships to it—though in the modern world it seems as if we have forgotten this. The manner in which we have chosen to operate within our societies is degrading these relationships, and thus jeopardizing the integrity of our physiological and psychological systems. The evidence for this degradation is clear if we choose to look for it, as are the means by which we can learn to reverse it.

A great example of the mass scale deterioration of a vital relationship to the earth is that of food and water. In order to be healthy in the body and mind we need to eat quality food and drink clean water. Without these things the body degenerates, as does the functioning of the mind; we become sick and stupid. Yet for some reason we continue to allow massive organizations working for the intention of profit to continually jeopardize humanity's relationship to quality food, and pollute drinking water through a variety of means. We can see this happening in the human macrocosm through industrial norms such the proliferation of GMO crops, on-going soil degradation through mono-cropping, the mass use of agricultural pesticides, hydraulic fracturing for natural gas, deep water oil drilling, open pit mining such as the Alberta oil sands, and the widespread economic disparity that forces a majority of the globe to starve in poverty.

On a smaller societal scale, we can also see examples of this deteriorating relationship in local governments shutting down or preventing sustainable food source and grey water recycling projects—like in September of 2012 when the City of Toronto, Canada ordered the destruction of a free public food garden the night before their harvest celebration, sending countless pounds of produce to the landfill in response to what they deemed unwelcomed public rebellion[1]. These are just a few examples of the destruction of our relationship to food and water, but this societal deterioration goes far deeper. There is a constantly growing body of evidence that exposes the manner in which we are destroying vital relationships to the Earth.

On a personal scale, the manner in which we are allowing society to be operated is cultivating an increasing disconnect from each other, the planet, and from an awareness of *self*. We are destroying the relationship to the very essence of human life; the sense of being loved. We can see this in the increasing rates of divorce, depression among adults and children, teenage suicide, and the dissolution of togetherness among people in general. The growing disconnection from a sense of being loved further perpetuates the personal and societal problems associated to it and this vicious circle continues to drill away at us. This is a problem within each of us, born of a degrading relationship to the intelligence of that which sustains us, best described at this time as *spirit*. It is a problem we need to face if we are to maintain the integrity of this planet for the generations to follow. Something inside of us needs to change.

We have got ourselves into quite a pickle here on planet Earth and each of us hold partial responsibility for the situation we are in. It may seem heavy for those who haven't already come to realize this, and the impending emotions that come with holding ourselves accountable to this responsibility can be very uncomfortable at first. It is these uncomfortable emotions that will play a vital role in regenerating the integrity of relationships to each other, ourselves, and to the planet. In learning to face these uncomfortable emotions, we learn a courage within, unmatched by any challenge from without. The general reluctance to face this accountability stems from a damaged relationship to *spirit*—the essence of life that connects all things. This connection may be the most vital for us to address at this time, as without it, we cannot cultivate the self-awareness and discover the courage needed to create lasting positive change. We have unconsciously allowed this damage to the integrity of our relationships over the generations and it is time we take the responsibility to heal them through reconnecting with *spirit*. But how do we learn to connect with something intangible, especially with generations of psychoemotional wounds that hinder us from doing so?

Across most cultures that have existed since the dawn of humankind, there has been the means to connect with *spirit,* and many used that connection to maintain the integrity of their relationships. The most historically common and generally effective means to cultivating this connection was through the ritualistic use of psychoactive plants or fungi as tools to reveal *spirit* directly, a means today that many refer to as shamanism. Loosely defined, shamanism is the practice of entering an altered state of consciousness for divination or healing. It has the potential to be extremely beneficial to us as individuals and as a society. Unfortunately, with shamanism often comes religious belief systems that one may be encouraged to subscribe to in order to gain its benefit. But it is the unchecked subscription to cultural belief systems that has placed us into the current problems we face. Without navigating these belief systems with a psychological model founded on a contemporary understanding, buying into shamanism may actually hold people back from the self-awareness needed to create lasting positive change, just as much as the detrimental belief systems of current society. So how do we make use of this valuable age-old practice without losing ourselves to incomplete cultural belief systems?

If we choose to look at shamanism as a means by which we enable an alternative perspective on *self* and the world, without fully buying into the cultural belief systems that may surround the practice, we can learn from altered states of consciousness without losing sight of the updated human knowledge base. This isn't to say we disregard these belief systems, as within them are many valuable tools for personal development and healing. I am suggesting we build new, more integral models on the use of psychoactive techniques, be they ancient or modern, which incorporate information from all ages and places. When we build these models, they can work like conceptual frameworks for navigating the experience of psychoactive substances more effectively. This enables us to integrate the alternative perspective they offer us more efficiently. In the time of great disconnect we are living in, I believe this alternative perspective could enable an understanding of how to heal damaged relationships, cultivate an honest connection with *spirit*, and create the lasting positive change we need to live abundant and healthy lives as individuals and as a global community.

I don't feel as though using psychoactive substances is for everybody, but the message they reveal within their use can be. **Decomposing The Shadow** is the presentation of an integral model for the experience of a powerful psychoactive fungus—*Teonanacatl*; the psilocybin mushroom. This book communicates the broadly applicable lessons revealed within the psilocybin experience in a way that is accessible, with or without having experienced these mushrooms directly. It offers those who have not explored the mushroom, and may never choose to, the opportunity to peek at the lessons it can offer us as a species. This book also offers a means for those who choose to explore the psilocybin mushroom to do so with a broader perspective of the psychology of the experience and how to navigate it in a manner that allows the experiences to be directly applicable to daily life.

Truly, the greatest risk of this mushroom is ignorant use, the exact type of use official drug education programs perpetuate through fear-mongering. It is my hope that this book offers the means for this ignorance to be dissolved, thus reducing the potential harm these powerful mushrooms can present. It is also my hope that this book offers a fuller picture on the sacredness of these mushrooms, so the trivialization they have suffered is removed from the cultural ethos. In doing so, I offer a map for personally regenerating one's relationship to *spirit* through psilocybin mushrooms, which in turn, may enable freedom from the conditioned societal belief systems destroying this relationship.

INTRODUCTION

This book outlines an experience that vastly transcends the normal conceptual realms of daily life, offering a psychological model for the experience of psilocybin mushrooms. It discusses the psychological processes that influence the unique characteristics of the psilocybin experience, and the broad-reaching implications it may have for understanding the nature of mind, emotion, spirituality, and life itself. In providing this model of the psilocybin-enhanced mind, it offers a map, or framework that allows people who choose to take this substance for personal growth to more effectively navigate the novel experiences it presents. Building this work has been a very challenging process for me, and I feel confident that the manner in which this information has been presented is widely accessible; however, there are a few points I feel are important to offer in advance.

Throughout the course of this book I refer to psilocybin mushrooms in a variety of terms—i.e., psilocybin mushrooms, the mushroom, psilocybin, magic mushrooms, mushrooms, etc. These are all references to the same substance and the variety in vernacular is intentionally chosen to keep the conversation fresh.

The flow of the book is structured very specifically. In Part 1, we initiate the conversation with my personal story. I feel it is important for the reader to know where I am coming from with this information and what has inspired me to present it. In Part 2, we disconnect from my personal perspective and enter an objective investigation into scientific and historical information regarding psilocybin mushrooms. The effort here is to create a rational foundation for the conversation that follows. In Part 3, we follow the trend of objective historical and scientific information and introduce anecdotal evidence to support the concept of psilocybin mushrooms as having spiritual potential. This concept is a vital element for this conversation and Part 3 is intended to offer a perspective on it from an accessible standpoint.

Part 4 gets into the full breadth of this work as I outline a psychological model, or framework, for psilocybin as it pertains to a full-blown spiritually psychedelic experience. Part 4 offers a variety of terms whose definitions and usage deviate from the cultural standard. In order to prevent confusion regarding these terms, they are clearly defined when presented and italicized throughout the book. Part 4 also makes several claims regarding the nature of mind, society, and health. These claims are supported where possible, but please read with constructive skepticism. I am not claiming I am right. I am simply offering what the psilocybin experience has communicated to me regarding these things.

Throughout this book I am presenting a perspective based on a certain caliber of experience with psilocybin; one that we are fully immersed within, but not so much as to be incapacitated from applying the lessons it may offer into daily life. Part 5 discusses different practices and perspectives I have found have allowed me a safe and effective potentiation of such an experience. This section is presented with the intention of harm reduction, and if one chooses to explore this substance, offers a means to enable the type of experience I am discussing here.

Part 6 offers some other concepts regarding the psilocybin experience that harmonize with the framework presented in Part 4, but didn't fit into the flow of information. With sections like "Nutritional Benefits" and

"Dagobah as a Proverb for the Psychedelic Journey", Part 6 explores a variety of different perspectives on psilocybin and psychedelics in general.

Part 7 is simply my closing thoughts; an attempt to tie together everything presented within this book into a personal, yet accessible, expression of *meaningfulness*.

The experiences occasioned by psilocybin mushrooms and by psychedelics in general are vast. They transcend the normal conceptual realms language allows us to understand them with. It is with this understanding I am acutely aware that I do not know the full picture of this experience. This book is like a two-dimensional snapshot of a multi-dimensional hologram; it is like a painting of a flower. It can never be the flower itself, but it can represent the artist's experience of the flower in a way that communicates inspiration and *meaningfulness* to others.

The repression of public investigations into the states of mind these substances unlock has greatly limited an understanding of them, and in turn, has limited the ability to apply that potential understanding to a fuller perspective of life itself. I hope this book can work as a referencing point by which we further investigate the potential of the human mind and what that potential has to show us about the nature of consciousness, our capacity for courage, honesty, and self-empowerment.

Enjoy.

PART 1: INITIATION

I was first introduced to "drugs" in the early 1990's through an elementary school program geared at indoctrinating kids with the rampant societal idiom of "Just Say No To Drugs". I still remember the day my grade school class was given our first "drug education". A female police officer came into the classroom and set up a bi-fold presentation board that displayed a literal pharmacopeia of illicit drugs. Until the next recess break, this police officer gave us the rundown of each of the drugs on her board, how destructive and horrible each one was, and a series of terrifying stories of lives "ruined" and families "destroyed". This process of instilling fear in children in an effort to prevent drug use is an unfortunately commonplace practice in Western society. I was young, and bought into this propaganda at the time. I was also a budding A.D.D. child and fascinated by the variety of colors and the different names for these drugs. I remember two particular drugs standing out most prominently for me: Magic Mushrooms and PCP. Thankfully as I grew up, the context of my life led me to the mushroom first.

I came home from school that day and said to my mother, "I might drink alcohol when I get older, but I will never do drugs"*. It's interesting to consider that statement now, in light of recognizing the level of

---

*I had all but forgotten of these ignorant words to my mother until she reminded me of them after I had been caught smoking Cannabis as a teenager.

miseducation that was being instilled into me at that time and throughout my life, the same societal miseducation my parents and many others are unfortunately still clouded by.

We are raised in a society whose perception of drugs is based on popular fiction more so than fact. We are indoctrinated into considering pharmaceuticals from the doctor as "good", alcohol, coffee, or cigarettes as potentially destructive but inherently "ok", and all drugs deemed illicit by the establishment as inherently "destructive", "life ruining", and "evil". These "morals" are continuously reinforced under the guise of protecting children, regardless of factual evidence. However, educating youth with this type of ignorant belief system towards drugs may ultimately present more of a problem than the drug use itself. When we educate children that the drugs which they will eventually be experimenting with are "destructive", "life-ruining" or "evil", we set them up to believe there is no way to utilize these drugs responsibly. By not giving people the opportunity to make informed choices, they will make ignorant ones. It took a lot of unnecessary mistakes for me to realize the drug paradigm I was indoctrinated into was based on broken logic and popular fiction.

With a constant growing base of evidence to support Harm Reduction[*] as the most effective form of drug education, it seems clear that the ongoing indoctrination of popular drug fiction over factual evidence is more about social control than cultivating responsible adults. There is nothing inherently "good" or "bad" about any given drug. Drugs are simply substances that can produce profound effects on the mind/body system. It is the experiences that come with those drugs, how those experiences may affect the general functioning of society[†], and how a person develops their relationship with those substances that determines their detrimental or beneficial potentials.

---

[*] Harm Reduction is a drug education paradigm that focuses on delivering the facts to people—both the good and the bad—and letting them make informed decisions, rather than providing only negative information and telling people to "just say no".

[†] If we ask the question, "Do the effects of this drug support or jeopardize the perpetuation of the status quo?", the answer will often help to elucidate the reasoning behind the societal value judgments given to a substance.

I had all but forgotten of the ignorant drug education I received as a child until I was reintroduced to the world of drugs through Cannabis at the age of 14. The softness I experienced with Cannabis at that age widened my understanding, and I realized what I had been told about this substance my whole life wasn't true. This ultimately caused me to question what else about drug education might not be true. I was reintroduced to Magic Mushrooms around 15 years old, but it wasn't until I was 17 that I tried them.

Throughout my childhood and all the way into my late teens, television played a huge role in helping my parents raise me—a situation I imagine many in my generation shared. In high school, television was the primary activity I took part in and one of the main reasons I never finished my homework. I did everything with the TV on. It was my friend, my confidant, and my parent in many ways. When I was granted free access to my father's computer, the Internet quickly joined television, becoming my primary role models, molding my self-image. My worldview was constructed from questions inspired by the TV, answers enabled through the Internet, and vice versa. Mass media culture was fashioning my mind and personality through these technologies, effectively cutting off my parents as my primary sources of guidance and wisdom—a blessing and a curse. A blessing, because my parents were stout Christians and these media offered me exposure to a world that existed beyond the safety bubble my parents had lovingly constructed throughout my childhood. A curse, because it left me scattered and without real human experience from a loved one to guide me.

Like any powerful first experience in life, my first exploration of the psilocybin space came with a powerful lesson. For reasons quite silly in retrospect but imperative at the time, I had my mother pick me up from a friend's place at the peak of my psychedelic experience. Thankfully, having never experimented with any drugs growing up, she wasn't able to spot any irregularity in my behavior. When we got home, she went to bed and I went to the basement to wait for a phone call from my girlfriend, who was vacationing in Florida. While I waited for her call, I began to feel terribly anxious. I tried to watch TV to distract myself, which normally did a great job at distracting me form uncomfortable emotions. I was flicking through the channels but everything on the television felt empty, hollow, and meaningless. I went to the computer to surf the Internet, hoping that would help calm me down. I couldn't think of anything specific to look up online, so I tried my favorite websites, but one after another, they were all meaningless too.

My two main emotional support structures were failing me and I began to be overwhelmed by a sense of emptiness I didn't understand. I was laying in fetal position on the basement floor in a cold sweat and felt like I was going to die. Synchronistically, just as I was approaching what felt like the apex of my impending death, my girlfriend called. I felt no solace in talking with her. In fact, somehow the conversation even became an argument*. Our phone time didn't go far and I was pretty quick to hang up and call the friends I had left earlier, pleading for them to come pick me up. They agreed to come get me and so I prepared myself to leave and got my younger sister, Jessica, to come lock the front door behind me.

My sister and I had a great relationship growing up; we were like best friends. But she is a couple years younger than me and when I hit my teenage rebel stage, we began to grow apart. In retrospect, I can only imagine how lonely she must have felt as her brother suddenly became a different person, stopped wanting to hang out with her, and was doing and saying things she didn't understand.

While standing beside her at the front door, still shaking a bit from my nearly complete emotional break, I became intimately aware of how much I appreciated and loved my sister†. Hugging her with more honesty than I could remember, I told her how much I loved her before walking out to my friend's van. I'll never forget her not-so-subtle awkwardness as she half-hugged me back, saying, "Uh... I love you too, bro."

---

* Oh, teenage relationship drama, how I don't miss you.
† Something I had forgotten in the midst of my conditioned male adolescent resistance to expressions of love and dependence.

It was not until much later in life that I began to recognize what I had actually learned that night. During my first experience with mushrooms, I was granted a conscious awareness of how hollow and mindless television and Internet entertainment could be. That awareness cracked the foundation of the roles they had been playing in my life at that time—but that experience was only the beginning.

Magic mushrooms became a vital part of my life during those early years of experimentation, but not a frequent one. I used them to have adventures and to go to parties, taking them if I wanted something stronger than cannabis or alcohol. I had some good times and some hard times, but for a long time, mushrooms were still only a "drug"; an immature means to entertainment and escapism. It wasn't until I found myself 23 years old and facing the truth of having lost control to destructive habits and selfish patterns, that I was in a position to understand the mushroom's true value.

I don't think it comes as much of a surprise—this idea that as we get older, we get a little more experienced, a little more self-aware of what we did and didn't understand about our actions and choices as a youth. When I was about 19 or 20, I decided to spontaneously leave my life in Ontario, move out of my parents' house for the first time, and head to Alberta, the other side of Canada. When I got there, I felt like I was becoming this whole new person—but ultimately, I didn't really change much. I was a beer drinking, record store working, pop culture fanatic young man. The real change in me came when I decided to leave for a backpacking adventure through Australia just after my 23rd birthday.

Shortly after getting to Australia, I became very sick. I was having intense fevers and serious gastrointestinal issues. In the midst of this illness I decided to head towards Melbourne. A friend's mother lived there and helped take care of me. After mostly recovering, she gave me the get-out-there-and-take-care-of-yourself boot. Another friend, who was among the closest people in my life while living in Alberta, was also living in Melbourne at the time. Through him, I met some wonderfully generous and welcoming locals who invited me into their lives. It was with those people that I had my first full-blown psychedelic experience: LSD.

My physical sickness had begun to fade in the time leading up to this psychedelic experience, but a depression was beginning to take a strong hold in me, and I didn't understand why. Initially, I had a lot of hesitance when I was offered this LSD. Like many of us growing up in the post-hippy paradigm, I was brought up to believe that LSD was the ultimate drug: using it once could "mess up your mind", there would be "no turning back", you would be locked into an "everlasting nightmare", and other fictitious stigma. I was afraid, but ultimately trusted these new friends, and together in a beautiful home, four of us shared an experience that changed me forever.

A lot happened for me during this experience, but the most important element of it came during a moment of deep, overwhelming depression. With my head in my hands, I was complaining about all the reasons my life was so hard, things like, "I'm not this, I'm not that. I can't do this, I can't do that", etc. Then, all of the sudden, I had an entirely new awareness. I was outside of myself, looking at myself. From this perspective I could see that I was causing my own depression by perpetuating an inner-narrative of self-deprecation and scarcity. I saw that I had the power to change this, and realized that I could remove the dissonance arising between me and my experience by letting go of my old story, "Canada James", and building a new story, "Melbourne James".

That moment empowered me into a sense of personal freedom like I had not known before. All bets were off. I was open to experiencing almost anything. Unfortunately, I led myself into a reckless lifestyle of recreational drug use and near constant partying. I won't pretend that I wasn't having fun, but it came with a cost. About eight months into this lifestyle, I began to recognize I had lost self-control and fallen into compulsive drug use. It seems cliché, but I woke up one morning after a long weekend and literally didn't recognize myself in the mirror. I had spent so much time basically unconscious to the implications of the choice to feed myself mind-altering substances that I had lost track of the person I was becoming. I didn't know who this new person was, and he was so different from the person I used to be, that I couldn't identify with either of them. I was suddenly immersed in the serious psychological consequences of my immature decisions and I had no idea what to do about it.

I felt lost, confused, regretful, and most of all, ashamed. What would my parents think? Again, it seems cliché, but I set off on a journey to heal myself and discover who I was when I wasn't immersed in the Melbourne lifestyle. The journey brought me across Australia, back and forth through Melbourne, throughout Southeast Asia, and eventually home to Canada to see my family again for the first time in 15 months. Back in Canada, I was freshly healing from a near complete psychological breakdown in Bangkok and was nowhere near stable. I was jumbled and confused, but thankfully grounded enough that this new James only mildly scared his friends and family. It was an incredibly challenging process of not only learning to make healthier lifestyle choices, but doing so in an environment with a lot of personal history. I was also discovering the self-destructive, self-judging, self-punishing, and self-deprecating inner-narratives that were negatively influencing my ongoing experience of life, and preventing me from being a confident, full person.

Throughout my travels, I had already begun to incorporate a variety of different healing practices in my life, including Reiki, daily meditation, and yoga, though I still felt psychologically and emotionally twisted. I felt myself fragmented from the inside out and needed help to become *whole* again. It may seem paradoxical, but I eventually decided I would utilize psychoactive plants as part of the spiritual practices I had implemented in my life. I read about the cultural history of their use for healing mental/emotional illness—the same type of illness I was suffering from—and I felt called to see if they could help me. I wasn't exactly desperate anymore, but I still felt this dull psychological ache. I needed to move through this ache and get on with my life, so I decided to see what these plants could do for me.

I already had this idea that psilocybin mushrooms had a spiritual potential based on the psychedelic philosophy I researched during my period of destructive use. At the time, my reasoning for researching these philosophies was an immature attempt at justifying my drug use. But later,

8

they would become the framework by which I was able to make mature choices and better understand the implications the psychedelic experience held for me and for life in general. Through this research, I made the decision that these mushrooms would be the right avenue for me to explore and heal the wounds and challenges I was discovering within myself; to help me move beyond my negative inner-narratives into a sense of clarity and confidence. I had no idea I was about to embark on a journey that would expose me to not only the deeper aspects of myself, but to the illusions upon which society is founded, to the depth of one's ability to heal oneself, and to how mushrooms can guide us through this process when we develop a strong relationship with them as a personal teacher and ally.

When I started exploring this new relationship with the mushroom, I wasn't following anyone's instructions. The choices I made in building my practice were based on a somewhat informed, albeit limited, understanding of how shamanic cultures derived significance from their use of psychoactive plants—such as *ceremony*, which is important as a self-regulatory system, and to establish one's intention of use. It was my awareness of the importance of *ceremony* that inspired me in cultivating my practice. I decided my *ceremony* would be held with the intentions of respect, opening myself up to learn, and letting go of my old definitions in favor of new understandings. I also wanted this practice to be associated with something larger than myself, such as the organic cycles of the planet. I decided my mushroom *ceremony*, which I called "full moon alchemy", would only take place once a month, and always on the full moon. This was also a great way to regulate my usage; maintaining a necessary frequency while allowing time between ceremonies to digest my experiences.

I started this practice in June 2010. During the first few sessions I had a friend come with me as a sitter. By the third month I started going alone, out into the night with only my senses and the mushrooms to guide me. I would go into an area of natural beauty, sit in meditation, and turn my awareness within. Throughout this practice I faced great challenges and processed some very dark emotions that I had been repressing my entire life—loneliness, anger, regret, sadness, shame, and alienation, among others. At the same time, I was also opening myself up to what felt then, and still feels now, like a direct connection with an aspect of myself best described as *spirit*. This practice helped me to develop a better understanding of not only myself, but of what the broader implications of the psilocybin experience may be. In contemplating it, I realized psilocybin was exposing me to previously unrealized perspectives on the nature of mind, cultural conditioning, emotional repression, the cultivation of personal courage, and the honesty of emotion. It was offering me a perspective on what it means to become *whole*.

I ended this practice after thirteen months in order to take a step back and look at myself. Before I began, I felt fragmented and confused. My deeper sense of confidence had slipped away in Melbourne when I realized I had become the opposite type of person I wanted to be; I had forgotten where I had been keeping my inner-light. Coming out on the other end of those thirteen months with the mushroom, I felt healed, *whole*, self-aware and in line with the deep passions firing my life forward. I do not attribute these changes completely to the mushroom, though I recognize it was their guidance that helped me better understand why I make the choices I do, and how these choices are responsible for my growth and healing. The mushrooms helped me to be aware of a series of emotional wounds set into my subconscious over the course of my life, and how to integrate the lessons that lay dormant within them.

This book is an expression of what I have come to see as the broad-reaching implications of the experiences occasioned by psilocybin mushrooms. I recognize this will not be universal and that certain people might not be able to immediately relate. My intention is not to change anybody's mind or claim "this is the way it is". I feel as though all theories of the mind are merely metaphors to describe experiences so deeply subjective, they are almost beyond the objective *language* we have to describe them. I am simply doing my best to communicate what I have learned in the hope that, in some way, it can help deepen one's understanding of the potential for self-healing and courage within both the psychedelic experience and life in general. My intention with this book is to share what I have learned about the mind and society in relation to a spiritual practice that included psilocybin mushrooms. It is an attempt to paint with *language* a picture of the relationship I have developed with the mushroom in all its parts—a relationship that continues to grow and evolve.

My hope is that this work will provide those who don't yet understand the mushroom's potential with a framework by which it can be understood spiritually and utilized responsibly. But I do not encourage anybody to choose to use this substance based solely off of what I present here. As Siddhartha, the Buddha said:

> *"Do not believe in anything simply because you have heard it. Do not believe in anything simply because it is spoken and rumored by many. Do not believe in anything simply because it is found written in your religious books. Do not believe in anything merely on the authority of your teachers and elders. Do not believe in traditions because they have been handed down for many generations. But after observation and analysis, when you find that anything agrees with reason and is conducive to the good and benefit of one and all, then accept it and live up to it.[2]"*

PART 2: AN OVERVIEW

STARTING OUT

Before we go into the conceptual framework for how psilocybin facilitates personal growth and psychospiritual maturation*, it is important for us to discuss some of the unique aspects of psilocybin mushrooms. My efforts here are to provide a very basic understanding of the roles these mushrooms have played throughout our history, and the manner in which they function within the body, for those who know little or nothing about them. Gaining an understanding of how psilocybin operates in the human system from a physiological perspective is an important element to exploring their significance. When we better understand the effects of a substance, we can relax more fully into the experience. When it comes to psychedelics, staying relaxed is a key component to cultivating their potential for psychospiritual growth.

What I am presenting here is a brief overview that includes the information I feel is relevant to establishing a solid foundation for the

---

* Psychospiritual Maturation is a term coined by Neal Goldsmith, Ph.D. It is the process by which one develops the ability to consciously and confidently embody the deeper essence of *self* into their identity by growing out of the psychological blockages that are preventing them from living out their true and unhindered *whole self* – something we will explore in more detail later.

content to follow. For a more complete overview of the history of psychedelics, there are many other books which will provide you a much deeper lesson, some of which you will find listed the bibliography of this book.

MAGIC MUSHROOMS - WHAT ARE THOSE?

'Magic Mushrooms' is a term used to describe a strain of mushrooms of the genus Psilocybe, which contain the alkaloids psilocin and psilocybin [3] (*4-hydroxy-N, N-dimethyltryptamine* and *O-phosphoryl-4-hydroxy-N, N-dimethyltryptamine*, respectively). Both psilocybin and psilocin are tryptamines that closely resemble a primary neurotransmitter in our brain, called serotonin. They are highly psychoactive and primarily interact with the serotonin 5-ht2a receptors in the brain[4].

Psilocin is a rather unstable compound and is usually degraded from the mushroom with heat or drying. Psilocybin, however, is incredibly similar yet highly stable and can survive the drying process. The difference between these two compounds is very minor. Psilocybin is essentially the psilocin molecule with a phosphorous group attached to it. When psilocybin is orally ingested, a digestive enzyme in the body called alkaline phosphatase shaves off the phosphorus group, or dephosphorylates that molecule, converting it into psilocin[5]. It then enters into the blood stream, and eventually, the brain.

The **Psilocybin Mushroom Vault** on Erowid.com lists some of the positive effects of these mushrooms as "creative, philosophical or deep thinking: ideas flow more easily", "intense feelings of wonder", and "life-changing spiritual experience"; neutral effects as "starring and rainbow patterns around pinpoint lights", "feeling more emotionally sensitive", "memories come to life", and "open and closed-eye visuals (common at medium or stronger dose)"; and negative effects as "dizziness", "confusion", and "mild to severe anxiety".[6]

Psilocybin mushrooms have a strong contemporary subculture and hold a long history of religious use among indigenous people in Mesoamerica. Based on archeological findings (such as the Tasili-n-Ajjer plateau in southern Algeria, where rock paintings were found dating between four and two thousand years old, depicting people dancing with fists full of mushrooms and others of groups running with mushrooms in their hands through geometric structures[7]), it is possible the history of this religious use may span across many different cultures and trace back millennia.

The Mazatec people inhabit a mountain range in the northeast of Oaxaca, Mexico called the Sierra Mazateca. They are one of the Mesoamerican cultures that have a long tradition of psilocybin mushroom use. In the Mazatec tradition, the psilocybin mushroom is called *Teonanacatl*, which is often translated as 'divine flesh'. They usually eat *Teonanacatl* as a family group and only ever at night, as they have found it to be most conducive to visionary insight. To the Mazatec, it is a medicine, a tool for healing the mind and the emotional being[8].

With the exception of the curandero, most members of the Mazatec community do not eat the mushroom very often[*]. The curandero is a member of the community who dedicates themselves to learning and understanding the *language* of the divine mushrooms and the mental-emotional state it inspires in them in order to help others along their journeys. The role is earned, not chosen by the individual, and the curandero's value is determined by how successful they are in their social role as healer, elder, and person of wisdom. During a ceremony with *Teonanacatl*, the curandero is often invited to join as a guide to ensure a safe journey[9].

Historically, this tradition was first encountered by Western civilization when the conquistadors began to observe the practices of

---

[*] In Western contemporary language, a curandero is often referred to as a şhaman, which is a cross-cultural reference to the role of *medicine man* or *woman*. The term originates from Siberia.

indigenous peoples during the Spanish inquisition. I'm sure you can imagine what it was like for these devout Catholic soldiers to observe people they viewed as savages eating fungus off the ground and calling it Divine. The Conquistadors were offended and disgusted; seeing it as a perversion, as pagan and inspired by the devil[10]. This began a long history of suppressing the mushroom cult to a point wherein its practices were pushed so deep into hiding that it was not discovered again until the early 1900s. Attention towards the mushroom reemerged in 1906 when an American botanist named Franklin Sumer Earle collected in Cuba the first official specimen of *Stropharia Cubensis*[11], which was later renamed *Psilocybe Cubensis*. This marked the Western academic world's first direct encounter with the mysterious *Teonanacatl*.

The profound effects of such an introduction would not echo loudly until the early 1950s, when an investment banker and amateur mycologist named R. Gordon Wasson was the first to partake in a Mazatec ceremony with the psilocybin mushroom[*]. In 1953, led by a curdandera named Marina Sabina, this vice president of JP Morgan was the first contemporary Westerner documented to have fully experienced what he called the "bemushroomed"[12] state and bring its story back to the Western world.

Wasson wrote many articles during this era about the potential for human use of psychoactive compounds throughout history, often with his colleague and friend Albert Hoffman[†]. In June 1957[13], an article written by Wasson titled **Seeking the Magic Mushroom: A New York banker goes to Mexico's mountains to participate in the age-old rituals of Indians who chew strange growths that produce visions**, was printed in Life magazine. This article sparked a public awareness, which would later become a near revolution of consciousness, within the Western world.

---

[*] For a very interesting and alternative history of R. Gordon Wasson, I encourage you to seek out an essay called *R. Gordon Wasson The Man, The Legend, The Myth* by Jan Irvin, 2012.
[†] Hoffman was a Swiss chemist who isolated the active alkaloid within the mushroom, psilocybin, in 1958 and who is also famous for the synthesis of LSD-25 in 1945.

In 1960, a Harvard professor named Timothy Leary Ph.D. took his first dose of Psilocybin while on vacation in Cuernavaca, Mexico. Upon coming back to the United States, he shared his profound paradigm shift with his colleagues and started a movement within Harvard that would be the first wave of the psychedelic '60s. By 1962, a group that included Leary, Richard Alpert Ph.D., and several graduate students, began a series of experiments called the Harvard Psilocybin Project. One of the most infamous experiments in the Psilocybin Project is the Concord Prison Experiment, where they investigated the use of psilocybin and psychotherapy to encourage a reduction of antisocial behavior outside of prison. Their conclusions from this experiment were determined by comparing the rate of recidivism[*] of those who participated in the experiments and those who did not. The results of the Concord Prison Experiment had seemed promising at the time, but inconsistencies in Leary's statements regarding its results and what later turned out to be little to no reduction in recidivism in the experimental group compared to the average prison population, caused a general disregard of his data[14], even though some of it still held important implications[†].

As time went on, tension started to grow between Harvard administration and Leary's group due to his growing support of unbarred psychedelic use and the establishment's fear of its destructive potential, eventually resulting in both Leary and his partner Alpert's dismissal from Harvard in 1963. This now famous event sent Leary and his group on a wild media ride throughout the '60s as he continued to publicly encourage psychedelic use through clever mottos and trickster-like antics such as his infamous catchphrase, "turn on, tune in, drop out." His voice and the actions that accompanied it, alongside many others such as Ken Kesey[‡],

---

[*] The tendency to relapse back into crime and be sent back to prison.

[†] For a deeper investigation into this experiment and the results, check out Dr. *Leary's Concord Prison Experiment: A 34 Year Follow-Up Study* by Rick Doblin 1998.

[‡] The Author of **One Flew Over The Cuckoo's Nest,** and responsible for a nationwide tour of exposing people to LSD through a group called the Merry Pranksters. The book **Electric Cool-Aide Acid Test** by Tom Wolfe explores their journey in detail.

was largely responsible for the dramatic uprising in psychedelic use — both constructive and destructive — among United States youth in the 1960's.

This era of youthful rebellion fuelled significant tension within the governmental system at the time. The emerging paradigm of the psychedelic culture was in direct opposition to the American establishment's political and economic focus, often manifesting as public resistance to the war in Vietnam and the military industrial complex in general. In fear of losing control, the government of the United States scrambled to protect their power and implemented the **Comprehensive Drug Abuse Prevention and Control Act** in 1970.

Though medical research at time showed psychedelics like psilocybin and LSD as having profound psychotherapeutic benefits, * all known psychedelic compounds, even those obscure and unpopular such as DMT (n, n-dimethyltryptamine) were criminalized under Schedule 1 of this act. This action was made out of a fear of losing control, by an establishment whose ability to maintain that control is based on a hierarchy of political power. A hierarchy held up by the ignorance and compliance of its population, which seemed to be disappearing from the people who had partaken in the psychedelic experience.

To be a Schedule 1 substance in the **Controlled Substance Act** of the United States, a substance must meet three basic requirements:

(A) The drug or other substance has a high potential for abuse.
(B) The drug or other substance has no currently accepted medical use in treatment in the United States.
(C) There is a lack of accepted safety for use of the drug or other substance under medical supervision.[15]

---

* The books **Psychedelic Healing** by Neal Goldsmith and **Psychedelic Explorer's Guide** by James Fadiman provide more in depth investigation into the various therapeutic potentials of psychedelics.

When we review the substances included in Schedule 1 of this act[*], we are given a clear example of the limited perspective held during the decision making process. Please remember that Schedule 1 states that a substance has "no currently accepted medical use in treatment"[16]. Along with psilocybin and LSD, other potentially beneficial substances that were banned include:

MDMA (Methylenedioxymethamphetamine) – Currently being researched with significantly promising therapeutic results for treatment-resistant post-traumatic stress disorder[17].

Ibogaine – Currently used in other countries to effectively treat severe drug addiction including Heroin, Alcohol, Methamphetamine, and Nicotine in a single session. It has also been shown to stop the physical withdrawal symptoms of Heroin within five hours of being administered[18].

Cannabis – Potential treatment for mental disorders, Alzheimer's disease, lung cancer, multiple sclerosis, leukemia, Parkinson's disease, sleep apnea, as an anti-inflammatory and for many other potential uses[19].

The scheduling of these substances in this fashion has greatly hindered, if not prevented, their medical value from being examined and utilized within United States and most other Westernized countries (whose laws are often influenced by the American Empire's political decisions) for decades.

ENTER MCKENNA

In 1971, a young rogue intellectual named Terence McKenna and his brother went with three others to a small village called La Chorrea in the South Amazon Basin. They hoped to study an elusive DMT-containing resin used among indigenous tribes called 'Oo-Koo-He'. Instead, they discovered the Stropharia Cubensis and underwent a dramatic series of transformative experiences[20]. This set of experiences inspired a strange and

---

[*] At the time of writing this book.

new worldview in McKenna, which led him and his bother to write two books that became famous to the psychedelic subculture: **The Invisible Landscape** (1975) which presented a complex theory of time cycles they called *TimeWaveZero* and 'novelty theory'[*], and **Psilocybin: Magic Mushrooms Growers Guide** (1976) under the pseudonyms OT Oss and ON Oeric, which introduced to the masses the ability to cultivate their own psilocybin mushrooms.

McKenna embodied a psychedelic paradigm based on intellectual inquiry, existential analysis, historical significance, creative poetic language and personal experience. This viewpoint was largely absent in the youth of the '90s, whose understanding of psychedelics was strongly limited by cultural stigma and ignorance. In 1992, McKenna's groundbreaking book **Food of the Gods** presented a detailed account of his perspective on humanity's long running history of symbiotic relationships with the planet through the use of mind-altering substances. In it, he addresses the hypocritical positioning of laws regarding psychedelic plants in relation to currently legal drugs such as coffee, sugar, and alcohol. He also provides a detailed account of the historical roles major governments have played in war, slavery, and economic manipulation using these drugs, among others. His book offers, what was at the time, a very new perspective on the history of drugs and our evolution as a civilized species.

In **Food of the Gods**, McKenna describes his Stoned Ape Theory, laying out historical and archeological evidence for psilocybin's role in human evolution. He hypothesized that after our pre-evolutionary ancestors were forced out of the canopy and onto the savannah by the drying of the African continent, they went out in search of new food sources to sustain them, sampling what they could in order to understand what was available. Among their experiments with new food on this vast, and at the time, wet land, they came upon psilocybin mushrooms growing

---

[*] These are incredibly complex theories and instead of trying to recapitulate them simply here, I suggest you check out *The Invisible Landscape* where it is explained in detail.

in the dung of cattle.

When our ancestors began to ingest psilocybin mushrooms and discover their evolutionary benefits, such as increased visual acuity[*], they began to integrate them into their diet. Through this process of integration they expanded their use, and their effects began to change us as a species. He proposes—based on the archeological evidence of mushroom imagery amongst prehistoric cultures as well as a personal understanding of the psilocybin experience—that it was these mushrooms that helped us to develop a self-reflexive awareness, language, and culture[21]. For more depth on this theory and the history of drugs in general, I highly suggest you investigate Terrence McKenna and his works.

McKenna gave lectures on his deeply inspired ideas about psychedelics and his poetic, enigmatic voice began to echo throughout the post '60s subculture of psychedelic intellectuals. To this day, there are still hundreds of available audio clips of his lectures on topics ranging from cultural history, post-humanism, UFO's, alchemy, DMT, consciousness, evolution, psychedelics, and the infamous Stoned Ape Theory.

Terrence McKenna died on April 3, 2000 due to a rare and severe brain tumor, but his ideas continue to inspire a whole new era of psychonaut youth. McKenna is by no means a psychedelic guru with all the answers, though the language he established to discuss the poetic nuances and existential implications of the psilocybin experience was of great benefit to my own process of maturing and understanding my relationship with the mushroom. He inspired me to contemplate what their spiritual and conceptual possibilities were, beyond the juvenile perspectives I was granted through my cultural upbringing. McKenna opened an entirely new paradigm for the implications of psychedelics and the nature of experience itself.

---

[*] In the context in which he references it, visual acuity is sharpness in vision or edge detection.

From purely botanical observations and indigenous ceremonies, to scientific research and contemporary usage, psychedelics continue to proliferate the cultural mind. McKenna helped continue a deepening dialog regarding psilocybin and psychedelics in general. His works and philosophy surrounding these substances have played a major role in the underground movement of psychedelic philosophy and psychology, yet it was only a stepping-stone for a deepening understanding of the dynamic implications these substances present. By investigating the realms of experience unlocked by these substances, we expand an awareness of ourselves and the nature of life itself. When it comes to psilocybin mushrooms, the realms of awareness it opens are those of spiritual self-discovery and psychoemotional healing.

PART 3: SPIRITUAL POTENTIAL

A DIVINE OPPORTUNITY

Since psychedelics have hit the scene in the Western world, the numbers and range of people who advocate their potential for catalyzing spiritual experiences—everyone from the average Joe to the trained scientist—has been expanding. For those who have never had a spiritual experience or explored psychedelic states of mind, or even for those who have without having a spiritual experience, this may be difficult to grasp. This book intends to translate the conceptual *language* I have learned to use to communicate with the spiritual potential of psilocybin mushrooms. Once we learn how to communicate with the mushroom in this way, I believe it will help to further unlock our potential for spiritual experiences.

Before we are able to discuss the spiritual potential of psychedelic substances, we first need to understand what 'spiritual' means, as it is a widely used but often vague term. The term 'spiritual', as I use it here, is in reference to a process, experience, or group of experiences that are in connection with *spirit*. Being the inner-essence of who we are, the ground of our being, the substrate from which our conscious lives emerge, our *spirit* is the aspect of us that exists before any of our learned behaviors, patterns, or values. Though the manner in which this *spirit,* or inner-essence, manifests in each one of us is as infinitely unique as our personality, it is an aspect of us that is universal throughout humanity. In that universality, it connects us all. Thus, spirituality is the quality of being spiritual, the quality of being of one's deepest inner-essence.

Psychedelics expose us to this inner-essence in a variety of ways, depending on the experiential characteristics of the specific substance we are using. The ability to connect with one's inner-essence is available through psychedelics in general, though it is not always the tendency of direction for every substance. Each variety of psychedelic substance varies in their degree of experiential spiritual connectivity, according to their respective characteristics. When we read into the scientific research and anecdotal evidence of psychedelics'—specifically, psilocybin's—potential for catalyzing mystical or spiritual-type experiences, we increase our ability to understand their spiritual elements and potentiate those elements into our experiences.

Beyond the history of the indigenous use of psychedelic substances we spoke of earlier, there are a handful different academic research studies and many different personal stories that provide evidence towards their spiritual potential. To better elucidate how the scientific findings and anecdotal evidence supports the potential for psychedelics to potentiate spiritual experiences, we will look at three significant cases that directly relate to psilocybin and its influence on psychedelic subculture.

THE GOOD FRIDAY EXPERIMENT

On Good Friday 1962, an experiment designed by Harvard theology scholar Walter Pahnke, M.D. was conducted with subjects training to become priests in the Marsh Chapel of Boston University. There were 20 participants, half of which were given psilocybin and the other half a placebo, Methylphenidate (Ritalin). Pahnke's intention was to see whether or not psychedelics produced an authentic mystical experience in the subjects. He chose to use psilocybin in his study because it—in the form of whole mushrooms—had been used historically in religious ceremonies among certain indigenous cultures.[22]

In the basement of the Chapel, the participants were able to hear the Good Friday sermon going on above them through a radio. They were confined to the room for the duration of the experience, and then surveyed one to two days afterwards. Pahnke and other theological scholars created this survey to rate the level of similarity between the experience of the participants and a "classically described mystical experience". Pahnke also submitted the participants' written accounts to a panel of theologians to be scored for authenticity. The general consensus of that panel was the experiences of the participants who had received the psilocybin that day were comparable to this classically defined religious or mystical experience. The placebo group's experiences were nowhere near comparable. In order for Pahnke to further confirm his observations, there was also a follow up with participants two months following the experiment.

After reviewing the surveys and the written experiences of the participants, Pahnke concluded the described experiences of those who received psilocybin during the experiment were indistinguishable from that of a traditional mystical experience. The participants echoed this conclusion, most feeling as though that experience was among the most spiritually significant of their lives. One of the Participants, Rev. Randell Laakko, when interviewed for a documentary entitled **LSD: The Beyond Within**, commented that regardless of whether or not it was an authentic mystical experience, it was still "deeply meaningful and moving"[23] to his life.

It is clear that the context of Pahnke's experiment was strongly inclined towards a religious theme, though it is important to note that his intention was not to produce evidence that psilocybin caused mystical experiences in general. His intentions were to discover the relevance of that experience in the context of a religious ceremonial environment, similar to those of indigenous use[24]. This setting-specific intention does play a key role in utilizing the potential of psilocybin mushrooms in a spiritual context, but not necessarily to the degree that Pahnke had established. The potential for psilocybin to produce such mystical experiences without a strong religious setting was conclusively addressed by Roland Griffiths nearly 40 years later.

GRIFFITHS AND A RESURGENCE OF MEDICAL RESEARCH

After paranoid decisions by the American federal government resulted in a complete ban on any research with psychedelics, these powerful substances all but vanished from the academic eye, apart from the occasional stigma-founded ridicule. This intellectual darkness lasted several years until a medical researcher named Rick Strassmann did experiments with DMT in the early '90s. The academic eye further cast its awareness onto psychedelics with research on psilocybin by Roland Griffiths at the turn of the millennium.[25]

Roland Griffiths is a Professor of behavioral biology and neuroscience, whose academic career is strongly supported by his research into the psychopharmacological relationships between drugs and animals[26]. Griffiths' intention with his experiments in 2006 was, "to see if psilocybin could occasion meaningful experiences of a spiritual type,"[27] based on the historical significance psilocybin mushrooms hold in the religious ceremonies of indigenous cultures, such as the Mazetoc. The main difference between his and Pahnke's studies was that he did not create a religious-specific setting. Instead, Griffiths created a comfortable and supportive environment to allow an easy passage through the experience, while allowing that experience to take its own course. He did, like Panhke, decide to use Methylphenidate (Ritalin) as the control substance in the double blind, placebo controlled experiment. The average age among the participants was 46, and they were all well educated with either a graduate or post-graduate degree. 53% (or 19) of the volunteer participants indicated an affiliation with specific religious or spiritual communities; however, all participated in religious/spiritual activities such as prayer, religious services, education or discussion groups, meditation, or church choir. Of these activities, 56% (or 20) stated their participation as daily, and 39% (or 14) as at least monthly.[28]

After the experiment, participants were given a 100-question survey. Of the 100 questions on the survey, 43 were directly from the Pahnke-Richards Mystical Experience Questionnaire used in the Good Friday Experiment. According to the outcome of the survey, 22 of the 36 participants given the psilocybin—or 61%—met the reviewer's criteria of a complete mystical experience.

At the two-month review, 67% of the participants rated their psilocybin experience to be either the single most meaningful event in their lives, or among the top five. In his paper, Griffiths states participants described the psilocybin experience as, "having substantial personal meaning and spiritual significance[,] and attributed […] sustained positive changes in attitudes and behavior consistent with changes rated by community observers", and concludes, "when administered under supportive conditions, psilocybin occasioned experiences similar to spontaneously occurring mystical experiences".[29]

Fourteen months later, Griffiths again reviewed all 36 participants' experiences. He found that of the original 22, 21 of the participants' accounts of their psilocybin experience still met the criteria of a complete mystical experience. None had rated the experience as less meaningful, and 58% (or 21) still rated it as among the top five experiences of their life[30,] feeling as though their psilocybin experience had benefited their quality of life. Griffiths and his team also interviewed members of the participants' immediate community for their observations of any change in the participants. He found that their observations often supported the participants' claims of having a higher quality of life after their psilocybin experience. With his continued research, Griffiths now believes psilocybin could be used to treat some psychiatric and behavioral disorders such as depression[31].

In a paper released in 2011, Griffiths discusses the observation that a single psilocybin experience can effectually change an adult's personality by increasing their *openness*[32]: appreciation for art, emotion, adventure, imaginative ideas, curiosity, variety of experience, and higher creativity[33]. This is a very interesting observation, as after the age of 25-30, it is largely believed an adult's personality is basically set for the rest of their life. From a scientific perspective, personality is commonly measured using five categories: openness, neuroticism, extroversion, agreeableness, and conscientiousness. Griffiths is still in the midst of a series of promising experiments regarding psilocybin, including a study examining the correlations between psilocybin and the practice of meditation[34].

Griffiths is not the only one currently doing important research on psilocybin. We are beginning to see a psychedelic renaissance in certain academic communities around the world, including work by Charles Grob M.D.. Grob's research is showing promising results on psilocybin's ability to successfully address the near-death anxiety of terminally ill cancer patients[35]. With the growing body of clinical evidence towards the potential psilocybin contains to catalyze positive life-changing experience, it's no wonder it has been used in religious ceremonies for so long.

ALPERT'S METAMORPHOSIS INTO RAM DASS

Richard Alpert, Ph.D. was a professor at Harvard University. He was a partner to Timothy Leary during the Harvard Psilocybin Project and was also dismissed from Harvard along with Leary in 1963 due to the controversy they had stirred up among media. Following the events surrounding his dismissal, and hoping to fully access the realm of spiritual self-understanding and existence that he felt the LSD experience provided a sneak peak into, joined Leary to participate in a series of independent experiments with LSD throughout the 1960s.

After a while, Alpert came to the realization that no matter how "high" he got, he always came down. So in an effort to discover a way to get high and stay high, he went to the most spiritual place he could think of: India. Through a series of synchronistic events, he met Bhagwan Dass, who led him to the Marariji, who became his guru. While training in yoga under the Marariji and another man named Hari Dass Baba, Alpert came to the spiritual self-understanding he sought and eventually returned to the United States with the new name Baba Ram Dass[36].

His famous book **Be Here Now** sparked a spiritual movement for many people—including myself—throughout North America and around the world, and continues to hold relevance to those who open up to the wisdom embedded in this big blue book. In **Be Here Now**, Ram Dass speaks of how taking psilocybin helped him become aware of the hollow existence he was living and the true spiritual being present within him. Ram Dass recaps this change in a short self-narrated online documentary about his spiritual path called **Love.Serve.Remember**. Prior to the following quote from this documentary, Ram Dass discusses what he considers his past *self*, before he had taken psychedelics. He describes this past *self* as considering himself the poster-boy for "successful man" and having everything he could possibly want in his life, yet was still often overwhelmed by anxiety and self-doubt.

"I think that the turn around came from my meeting Tim Leary and my work with psychedelics. I was feeling very dissatisfied with psychology. It wasn't describing what was happening in my heart, and I had a psychoanalysis and that wasn't satisfying either. Then psychedelics gave me a new consciousness from my heart, it freed me from my roles. Before psychedelics I was just a set of roles, nothing behind it. The role of professor, role of lover, role of cello player, collector, the role of scientist. They didn't add up to a feeling of home, of being somewhere in myself and I was constantly looking at other people's eyes to see whether I was doing good. Psychedelics brought a

huge change. The [...] psilocybin mushrooms those made me realize that I was in reality down here, in my heart and not in my head. I was down here in a spiritual identity. Not in my ego which was based on fear [...] and the heart me was based on love [...] And I felt freed from other people's judgments of my actions."

- Baba Ram Dass[37]

Ram Dass is a beautiful example of how the experience of psilocybin mushrooms can dramatically change people for the better, opening them up to the spiritual essence buried deep beneath their cultural roles. With that being said, it is easy to become an evangelist for their potential, as many whom have "seen the light" of psychedelics do.

Psychedelics are not necessarily 'The Way'; they are more like a borrowed map. They may give us deep insight into *self* and enable us to process whatever may be holding us back from being the fullest expression of who we are. Unless those insights and changes are embodied into one's everyday life through methods that do not involve psychedelics, however, their power is lost.

Psychedelics are not for everyone. And like any spiritual technique or method, for some, they may be useful only up until the time they succeed at giving them what they had been seeking. After this point, it might be time to transcend, expand, or release from that stage of life. For others, however, these substances may become trusted allies in a spiritual practice, like they did for me. It is up to you to determine your relationship to them. Psychedelics are but one piece in a much larger puzzle, regardless of how you choose to utilize them. The following content serves to provide deeper insight into their potential, given the growth I have personally made as a result of my experiences with them.

PART 4: A CONCEPTUAL FRAMEWORK

LANGUAGE AND REALITY

LANGUAGING EXPERIENCES INTO FUNCTIONAL INSIGHT

As creatures of self-aware thought and higher cognitive function, our ability to *language* is a vital element of our ability to conceptualize our experiences. This is to say that our ability to integrate the implications of a given experience—be it personal, social, or existential—is relatively determined by our ability to *language* that experience. For most people, this *language* is verbal, but can be structured in any form of *syntax*[*], formal, or informal (i.e., philosophy, poetry, music, religion, visualization, art, dance, etc.).

If we lack the *syntax,* or the ability to associate a *language* to particular elements of an experience, the rational mind will often omit those particular elements in order to maintain the status quo, or normality, of an experience in accordance with our *languaging* capabilities. The

---

[*] For the purposes of this text, *syntax* refers to the amalgamated potential of our *languaging* capabilities.

omitted elements of that experience are thus unavailable to be consciously integrated as *functional insight**. In other words, if we lack the *syntax* to explain an experience to other people or to ourselves, we are less likely to fully grasp an understanding of its full implications. And, if we do not understand an experience, we cannot learn from it.

Thus, the first step in learning how to harness the potential of psilocybin is to establish a *language* that works as a conceptual framework for understanding; explaining and integrating the various elements of the psilocybin experience into *functional insight*. This book, in general, offers the *language* I have learned to incorporate into my *syntax*. This *language* has enabled me to cultivate a relationship with the mushroom that has allowed me experiences of psychospiritual healing on a more consistent basis.

LANGUAGING A PERSONAL TEACHER

In the general subculture of psychoactive plants and psychedelic drugs, the term *teacher* is often used to describe a certain substance. But what exactly does this mean? How is it a teacher? What is the method by which it is teaching us? And what are the qualities of its lessons? In order to understand the terminology of 'teacher' and thus better understand the psilocybin mushroom's potential to play a *teacher* role, we need to investigate these questions, among others. The content of the following section establishes a verbal *language* to integrate a perception of psilocybin mushrooms as a *teacher*. It provides a conceptual framework for the various ideas and terms that may be used to describe psilocybin as such. Each major term will be italicized for clarity.

Psilocybin mushrooms are living organisms that inherently possess the ability to stimulate vast changes in perception when working symbiotically

---

* *Functional insight* can be looked upon as an insight, epiphany, or revelation that one can directly apply to one's life as a whole.

with a highly evolved consciousness, such as our own. When broken down in the digestive system, they expose the body to the alkaloids psilocybin and psilocin, which are both tryptamines[38]. Tryptamines are part of a class of chemical compounds called monoamine alkaloids that affect the functioning of the brain. Certain tryptamines, like serotonin and melatonin are very significant to the functioning of our physiological and psychological systems. Serotonin and melatonin are both endogenous (produced within our bodies) and play key roles in our regulatory systems. Serotonin is a very important neurotransmitter that affects mood and cognition. Melatonin is a hormone that regulates our sleeping patterns in response to perceived light levels[39].

The chemical process of psilocin* metabolizing through the brain takes us on a profoundly different experience of consciousness, altering our emotional and psychological reactions to every facet of life. It is this biochemical process in the brain that guides the psychedelic experience. In terms of the mushroom being a *teacher*, this process is like their *guidance*.

At a medium to higher dosage, which will be discussed in detail later, the mushroom *teaches* by stimulating an experience wherein our emotional potential† is turned up to full capacity; wherein we are exposed to emotional states beyond anything experienced in "normal" everyday consciousness. We are taken on a journey through the emotional being and shown how that emotional aspect of *self* understands itself and the world. This journey, often referred to as a psychedelic trip, is the change in how we see ourselves and the world that results from this biochemical process. By *guiding* us into potent psychoemotional states of awareness during a psilocybin trip, the mushroom enables insight into previously unknown levels of the emotional and spiritual *self*. These amplified states of emotional potency are like a *classroom* where we are able to directly

---

* As explained earlier, psilocybin is converted into psilocin in the body and is the primary alkaloid responsible for the visionary experience of mushrooms. Throughout this book I will often reference the experience with the word 'psilocybin'. This is a reference to the psilocybin mushroom as a whole, not necessarily as the exact psychoactive molecule behind the mushroom experience.
† The potential intensity of one's emotional experience.

explore the various implications of these psychoemotional states as they apply to our lives.

With the emotional and spiritual foundation of psilocybin-induced altered states, comes highly intellectual thought patterns that change the quality of one's inner-monologue. These thought patterns are directly stimulated by the newly altered perception of external and internal environments. These new thoughts come like transmissions of information received subjectively through our interaction with the external environment, now flavored with these psychedelic states of emotional and spiritual awareness. These thought transmissions are like the *teaching voice* of the mushroom.

There is a very distinct difference with how our inner-monologue works in this altered state. It often sounds less like one's own voice speaking by one's own efforts, and more like an external or exogenous intelligence communicating through one's mind. It is in this communication through our inner-monologue that we learn *lessons* about the *self* and the world. This seemingly exogenous inner-voice could be the intelligence of the mushroom speaking through the inner-monologue. It could also be the mushroom enabling direct communication with an element of the psyche normally so unconscious it feels external when it begins to communicate with the conscious mind. Or, it could be some combination of both, or neither. I don't think it really matters which of these are the case, as long as one actively chooses to recognize that what is being offered within this experience is deeply personal and honest.

It is important to remember that the way we regard the psilocybin experience will determine how deeply personal that experience—and thus the potential lessons within that experience—will be. The depth of *emotional potential* revealed to the conscious mind within the psychoemotional states unlocked by psilocybin becomes the perspective by which we perceive our environment*. This new perspective becomes a spiritual and emotional point of reference by which we

---

* We could also apply this concept to the perception of one's internal environment.

contemplate the external stimuli we are taking in with our physical senses, drastically altering the quality of the information we are processing. The more reverence and personalization we give to the psilocybin experience, the more emotionally and spiritually visceral the point of reference for our experience, and thus perception of our environment, will be. And, the deeper the point of emotional reference by which we perceive our environment, the deeper the potential *lessons* within those aforementioned thought transmissions will be.

The *lessons* we learn in our psychedelic experiences with psilocybin are relative to whatever psychospiritual challenges we may be facing at that particular time—whether those challenges are obvious to the conscious mind or not. The psilocybin mushroom interacts with the psyche to expose the emotional states necessary to address these unique challenges. The mushrooms *guide* us into those relevant psychoemotional states and communicate the significance of those states in a unique and seemingly magical way. This is how they act as a *teacher.*

The significance of the emotional states we enter with psilocybin is not usually communicated in the familiar form of words and sentences. It is communicated through creative ideas and metaphors, constructed on a personal symbolism. It is as if the *lessons* we are learning are found in the underlying moral of a metaphor representing the challenges we are facing within our personal process of psychospiritual maturation*, created out of an interaction between the psilocybin mushroom and our psyche. Which means, in order to understand the *lesson*, we must examine our experiences and the personal meaning of the symbolism presented. We must *language* these experiences in order to integrate them into our *syntax.*

With time and practice, we develop the ability to understand the underlying lessons of these experiences and become more familiar with the

---

* Psychospiritual Maturation is a term coined by Neal Goldsmith, Ph.D. It is the process by which we develop the ability to consciously and confidently embody the deeper essence of our *self* into our identity by growing out of the psychological blockages that are preventing us from living the true and unhindered *whole self* – something we will explore in more detail later.

deeper aspects of our *self*. The lessons become more straightforward and we become more able to understand what the symbolism in these experiences means on a personal level. There are infinitude different metaphors and potential experiences that can come from psilocybin, as each one of us has a vast and unique psyche. Yet, I believe there are underlying patterns of objective continuity or archetypal lessons and processes present within the psilocybin experience. These archetypal lessons and processes are not independent; but instead blend into each other seamlessly within the experience. They are also not inherently available to everybody, as many of us are bogged down by culturally conditioned psychological boundaries that effectively limit the potential depth of the psilocybin experience and life as a whole. These culturally conditioned boundaries, which limit one's psilocybin experience, paradoxically are the same boundaries that the psilocybin experience helps to dissolve and redefine. This boundary dissolution and redefinition generates an effect that ripples its benefits throughout our whole experience of life.

FREEING OURSELVES FROM CONDITIONED LANGUAGE

At the beginning of Part 4, we discussed the nature of *language* as a cognitive system used to construct a conceptual grasp on one's experiences, and how the sum potential of all personal *languaging* capabilities is called *syntax*. This book provides a *language* that one can be incorporated into the *syntax* to more effectively navigate the conceptual realms associated with psychospiritual healing and the psilocybin experience. Syntax is instilled and limited by the cultural environment of one's upbringing, cultural conditioning. What will be discussed here is an overview of how that culturally conditioned *syntax* places boundaries on one's potential experience of life, while also addressing how the mushroom can work to clear those unconscious boundaries through expanding *syntax* in a very unique and personal way. When used with directed intention, the mushroom can help free one from the psychoemotional limitations of cultural conditioning.

38

As infants, our brains are highly responsive, malleable, and eager to learn. In the earliest years of life, the brain begins to take on the complex process of establishing its neurological architecture as we learn and integrate lessons from physical and social environments: lessons about the world we are in and the relationship we have with its multiple elements[40]. During this process, we are taught the native *languaging* framework of our parents. Over time, this initial *language* learned during the earliest stages of life—used to describe the world we are interacting with so we can communicate and share our subjective experiences with others—becomes the foundation of *syntax:* our primary belief system, the point of reference by which we emotionally relate to the world, how we conceptualize experiences, and navigate reality. Throughout life, *syntax* develops without substantial deviation from its original form unless it is actively altered.

Western civilization educates its youth through a written tradition based on a verbal *language;* wherein the relationship to one's experience of the world, and of *self,* is mediated through the use of words or labels possessing a culturally predetermined *meaningfulness.* Over time, our brains become programmed to immediately *language* experiences with these culturally determined labels. We immediately think 'tree' or 'red car' or 'police officer' as soon as we are subjected to those elements within the environment. The *meaningfulness* of each label is defined by the cultural value of one's native *language* and these cultural values determine the manner in which we emotionally relate to those labels.

The brain immediately *languages* the elements of one's experiences with these culturally weighted labels, thus the default experience of reality is one of interacting with labels that represent cultural values. Although these immediate labels may be accurate in some sense, they are incomplete, as each element in our environment could play a myriad of potential roles. And since this label-based *language* is the primary means by which we are trained to interpret reality, this *language* limits the experiential characteristics of life. Instead of interacting with the dynamics of potential *meaningfulness* within reality, we are only interacting with a mirage of culturally weighted labels, superimposed over the experience of reality. We emotionally react to these labels, often unconsciously, rather than allowing the fullest potential of our experiences. The caliber of this labeling process is an expression of cultural conditioning, and if it is not expanded or transcended can lead to a very narrow and, in many cases, inaccurate worldview.

Let's look at an example of how this cultural conditioning influences one's reality by considering the label 'police officer'. In a well-to-do community where the police are (supposedly) responsible for safety and protection, people often understand the connotations associated with the label 'police officer' to be of helpfulness and compassion. Thus, they emotionally react to the culturally predetermined *meaningfulness* of this label, rather than the direct reality of the given situation. However, to people in the lower strata of the socio-economic hierarchy, who are constantly harassed by police, whose friends and family are also harassed, assaulted or arrested by police, the connotation of the label 'police officer' in their *syntax* will not be one of safety and protection, but one of control, malevolence, and aggression. They will only see a police officer as a tyrant and emotionally react accordingly.

Though both these definitions are applied to the same label and may be equally valid in their own context, they are vastly contrasting—a difference stimulated by a different cultural foundation influencing the perception of what the label 'police officer' means. This conditioned perception of the role of the police officer clouds one's ability to see beyond this conditioning when presented with a different context. This cultural conditioning extends its influence beyond how we perceive the elements in the external environment and also affects how we view our *self* and process emotion.

Cultural conditioning heavily influences the *languaging* potential of *syntax*. And the potential of *syntax* heavily determines the characteristics of our personal experiences from within, and that which we see as potential outside ourselves. If *syntax* lacks the ability to explain particular elements of one's experience, the conditioned mind will automatically omit those elements from conscious awareness in order to maintain the conceptual status quo of conditioned reality. Since most of us have been trained to think primarily with the *language* of verbal labeling and apply a culturally conditioned *meaningfulness* to those labels, the limitations of a cultural *language* become the limitations of personal *syntax,* and determine our capacity to contemplate the dynamics of life.

These cultural limitations hinder the ability to understand certain elements of *self* because we lack the *syntax* to explain it conceptually. If we only possess the culturally conditioned *syntax* embedded at infancy, we will lack the ability to contemplate ourselves beyond the confines of what is culturally determined. Without the *syntax* to contemplate our true potential, not only will we be limited in contemplating it, but also limited from ever manifesting the fullest expressions of that potential. Consider the previous example regarding 'police officer' and apply the same concept to the perception of personal success. What distinct experiential differences would we see between someone from a well-to-do community and someone from a low-income community? How would those differences in culturally predetermined *language* affect their perception of potential for personal success?

We are beginning to see how important it is for psychospiritual development that we identify and transcend the limitations of cultural conditioning. Yet, due to the conditioned mind's omission of any perceived element that does not fall in suit with the culturally determined status quo, we will not be able to perceive the limitations of *language* until *syntax* is expanded. Only when the culturally conditioned and impulsive inner-labeling is removed long enough to consider *self* and environment beyond the fundamentality incomplete, preconditioned cultural values bred into us, will we be able to transcend its conceptual hold on our experiences of life.

Another element of life that is limited by cultural conditioning is emotion. Emotions are aspects of experience that exist so deeply within, that their true significance transcends the *language* of verbal labels most have been taught to describe them with. Since one's *languaging* capabilities determine one's ability to conceptualize and thus directly integrate the elements of experience, the limited abilities of *language* can

41

work to circumscribe one's emotional understanding.

Verbal *language's* inability to fully conceptualize emotional experience limits emotional understanding in two ways. First, by limiting the ability to truly communicate our emotions to others, which often leaves us feeling alienated, confused, and can create a downward spiral of emotional instability. The second, is by shutting off the ability to experience emotions for what they truly are, enclosing us within that which we are able to *language* them as. The conditioned mind omits experiences that do not accord to the status quo reality and thus omits elements of emotions from conscious awareness. These emotions don't go away. They are unconsciously suppressed and begin to pile up within us. This suppression drastically hinders the ability to understand and process those emotions, the potential result of which can manifest as a variety of different psychological and physiological issues.

We are unable to effectively process the broader *meaningfulness* of emotions through verbal *language* because it can only address a small section of their value. With a *syntax* founded on the *language* of culturally determined verbal labels, we are boxed into a limited and incomplete understanding of our deeper emotional existence. This disconnection from directly understanding our emotions, founded in cultural conditioning, is a root cause for the psychosocial dissonance in human societies.

This cultural conditioning is by no means static. We are constantly growing, changing, and developing *syntax,* as individuals and as society at large. There are multiple ways to unlock emotional potential and get to a deeper understanding of the emotional *self.* Yet how can this be accomplished if the foundation of *syntax* is a culturally conditioned verbal *language?* One example, poetry, helps to expand *syntax* by exercising the ability to use verbal labels in an abstract manner. Another example is music, which allows a person to express themselves through the creation of a harmonious grouping of sounds. These are only two examples of how we can utilize an abstraction from normative cultural values in order to redefine the potential *meaningfulness* of experience itself.

Art in general is an effective method for processing unconsciously suppressed emotions. The process of creating art is an externalized expression of an internal state of being; it is a great way to connect with our emotional potential and practice non-verbal self-expression. Yet, in order to alter the mental system that is perpetuating the emotional suppression, we need to expand the ability to actually *feel* those emotions in the moment. This means we must alter the *languaging* process and allow emotion to flow so dramatically it forces an expansion of *syntax*. Once we unlock that direct emotional experience, we are able to contemplate ourselves beyond cultural conditioning and thus integrate the previously omitted elements of experience into status quo reality. This allows us a deeper experience of life.

There are methods other than the personal expression of creating art that facilitate the expansion of *syntax*, methods founded on externalities that provide a new set of values for our established verbal *languages*. Conversations with people that cause us to question our values, moving to a new city with a different set of cultural values, or going to school where we are subjected to new modes of thinking through intellectual study, are all examples of externally mediated *syntax* expansion. These externally founded methods are effective to some extent, though many of them only work to expand *syntax* through the same method that created it, by establishing an internal point of reference influenced by verbal labels founded on cultural values. These externally generated manners of expanding *syntax* may unlock the potential to contemplate existence more diversely. However, if these methods lack inspiration by deeply personal experience, they will not unlock a *language* that fully conceptualizes our deeper emotional existence.

A more effective method of expanding *syntax* is to push oneself into direct and intensely personal experiences that transcend any *language* previously available to describe it, a transcendental experience. If we return from this kind of experience with the intention to understand it, we are forced to expand upon previous *syntax* by creating a new and personal *language* that describes our relationship to this new experience. The expansion of *syntax* in this context is self-generated and thus holds more potential to be personally empowering.

Psilocybin mushrooms—when used in the conscious manner described here—can facilitate this type of transcendental experience. They cause an alteration in the perception of reality that is beyond what would be available through any typical biochemical operation of the brain. Mushrooms open the floodgates of emotional potential and can expand awareness beyond any *language* the cultural norm offers. When we *surrender* the conceptual control of the conditioned mind and enter the depth of emotional being unlocked by the use of psilocybin mushrooms, in the right setting, we can enter an emotional awareness of *self* and environment that far transcends the cultural status quo. This experience is stimulated from within and is completely unique to the subjective observer. It takes us beyond cultural conditioning and allows an opportunity to see the world through unconditioned eyes.

Psilocybin mushrooms awaken us to the opportunity of freeing ourselves from the limitations of cultural conditioning by expanding *syntax*. By allowing us to explore the deep emotional potential of ourselves, they also awaken us to the opportunity to process and heal a lifetime of suppressed emotion—a process called *emotive-psychosynthesis*. Once processed and conceptualized, these suppressed emotions will no longer create the same level of dissonance in the experience of life. We become uplifted and clear, self-empowered, and more open to beauty.

This book offers the *language* that allowed me to generate these types of psychospiritually healing experiences within my personal journey, and could help you generate them too. These types of experiences are very deep-seated and not always fun. Sometimes they may be brutally honest, such as when *facing the shadow*—an experience often tied to *emotive-psychosynthesis*. These deep-seated experiences may be very challenging, but can profoundly benefit our lives, and as a result, have a profoundly beneficial effect on the world at large. With time and practice, the deeply personal experiences occasioned by psilocybin mushrooms can become a point of reference we identify with throughout our experiences in life, completely unique and not determined by limiting cultural values. When this change occurs, we begin to create identity and label the elements of life through reference to an unconditioned emotional experience, our visions and dreams, instead of the *language* of mass culture. The world could gain greatly from more individuals taking on such a personally empowered perception. But like I said before, in order to get there we may have to face brutal honesty, an experience containing great healing and potential benefit.

SURRENDER

THE PROCESS OF SURRENDER

When the full-blown psychedelic state of psilocybin mushrooms blooms into our awareness, we are not left with much conscious control of our thoughts and emotions. Its presence comes on like a rushing waterfall and any attempts to circumvent its fullness are futile. If we do not give in to this powerful flow of energy we potentiate an unnecessary anxiety, often generated out of the conditioned mind's resistance to its own dissolution*. To give oneself into the oncoming emotional honesty of the psilocybin experience is the process of *surrender*.

Psilocybin mushrooms open the floodgates of the inner-universe, the emotional and spiritual aspects of *self*, bringing the truth of what is happening at the depths of who we are to the surface of awareness. Though overwhelming in certain contexts, this energetic rush is an expression of the deeper *self*, an expression of something within. This means that to *surrender* into the dynamic and amplified emotional experience of the psilocybin mushroom is to *surrender* to the deeper aspects of the

---

* I believe many "bad trips" come from holding too firmly to this relative perception of "I'm not sober" or "I'm not in control" and subsequently creating anxiety by resisting the state of mind one is in.

subconscious mind, both the light and the dark.

Psilocybin mushrooms amplify an awareness of the emotional *self*, enabling a broader view of the emotional and spiritual foundation of being. This, in turn, can present us with many things we may not wish to deal with; an awareness to elements of *self* we may not consciously wish to be exposed to, such as the *shadow* or dark side (an experience we will discuss in detail in the next chapter). But the mushrooms can also open us to experiencing an aspect of *self* that is divine or immaculate in nature. This aspect of *self* is a caliber of cognizance wherein we posses the ability to see profound beauty in ourselves and in others, to feel appreciation for life, or to be utterly amazed by what the natural world has to offer.

When we learn to actively release the conditioned mind's control within an altered state, to *surrender* the ego to a broader view of *self* and the worldview that psilocybin can bring about, these unlocked perceptions of emotional depth can be integrated more directly. In *surrender* we cease resisting the emotional intensity of the experience and allow it to flow through us freely, taking the negative pressure of conditioned resistance off of the conscious mind. This helps to develop the various elements of that experience into *functional insight*. As *functional insights* arise from the direct experience of the deeper elements of *self*, they help to generate a consciousness founded on a more dynamic experience of our *whole* being throughout everyday life, cultivating a more holistic self-awareness.

The expression of holistic self-awareness generated through the process of *surrendering* to the emotional honesty of psilocybin experiences becomes the new point of reference by which we experience life. This self-awareness takes precedence over the point of reference established by the psychological conditioning of our cultural environment. For me, the perspectives of the world and of myself that arose from the experience of *surrender*, in both psilocybin experiences and my life in general, have helped to free me from a zombie-like state, bred of the contemporary North American television culture in which I was raised.

Surrendering to the flowing psychedelic abundance that psilocybin awakens within the conscious mind can result in us developing a broader experience of *self* and of life in general. It can help to free us from the conditioned patterns of cultural upbringing. With the expanded dynamic of self-awareness and self-understanding, it can inspire a lasting sense of coherence within us. When living with that sense, we feel a direction and purpose, and when it is earned through a challenging experience like that of *surrendering* to the emotional intensity of psilocybin, we gain a deep recognition of having earned it.

> *"Personal coherence, also known as psychophysiological coherence, refers to the synchronization of our physical, mental and emotional systems. It can be measured by our heart-rhythm patterns: The more balanced and smooth they are, the more in sync, or coherent, we are. Stress levels recede, energy levels increase [in] our brain and what HeartMath calls the "heart brain" are working together. It is a state of optimal clarity, perception and performance."*
> *-The HeartMath Institute*[41]

SURRENDER, ANXIETY, AND THE SYNCHRONISTIC FLOW

Much of the anxiety we suffer in contemporary Western society comes from being unable to release the psychological control we attempt to maintain over events we cannot actually control. We attempt to maintain as much control of our environments and of ourselves as possible, yet as we grasp tighter and tighter, more and more, it slips through our fingers. We can see a great example of this in governments and corporations around the world, as they attempt to garner tighter control with surveillance, security forces, and censorship across the private and public sectors, through both physical and digital means. They are so afraid of losing control that they tighten their grip, only to see more people realize this and slip out of their grasp.

When we learn to *surrender* to the intensity of the emotional and spiritual rush psilocybin occasions, we learn a skill that functions across many different aspects of life. We can learn the fundamental skill of recognizing, "there is nothing I can do about this right now, so I might as well step back and learn something while doing my best to be easy on myself". We learn to release ourselves into the flow of things unfolding around us with non-passive acceptance. This is an essential skill for reducing anxiety in our everyday lives, thus increasing emotional stability, physical health, and general well-being.

Learning to adapt the skill of *surrender* into the daily flow of my life has increased the frequency in which I experience *synchronicity*. First presented and described by psychiatrist Carl Jung, *synchronicity* is the experience of realizing a series of coincidences so deeply meaningful and personally significant, they defy being simply coincidence. It is a caliber of alertness that directly correlates the seemingly unrelated flow of external events into a personally meaningful experience of wonder. Like that of psilocybin, it is an experience that blurs the lines separating the inner and outer world. It seems as though once we *surrender*, allowing an understanding of the way things are without the personal abstractions of what we want, we begin to connect with a sentience of how interconnected the flow of reality really is. This sentience, like the mushroom experience, changes the point of reference from which we move forward into the world, now more in line with the *synchronistic flow of life.*

The process of *surrender* has worked like a tool to unlock my ability to connect with this *synchronistic flow of life.* Relieving me of the psychologically conditioned, self-policing processes of controlling my personal world, it has offered me a way of seeing the grander cycles at work that both nourish and support me. This has been a wonderful and spiritually fulfilling change, and has added a flavor of magic to my life that is hard to describe without poetry.

God and Surrender

Surrender also plays a key role in facilitating deep mystical experiences. When open to receiving the true breadth of inner-essence through the psychedelic experience, we can allow the temporary dissolution of the ego function, which separates the conscious mind from deeper existence. This allows for the possibility to experience a deep, primordial, and universal aspect of *self*, the fullest potential of divine emotional creativity. We open ourselves up to "God".

The term 'God' means many things to many people and holds a lot of emotional and cultural weight. I know of many people that, due to their cultural upbringing and personal identifications with belief systems, have already made up their minds about what this term means to them and may not be interested in changing that. Since 'God' is a term with such a convoluted spectrum of potential *meaningfulness*, when I use *God*, it refers to the unfolding universe in its absolute completeness and the divine creative energy that sustains it: *All That Is, All At Once.*

There is a point within us where we connect with the *All That Is, All At Once.* This point is where our consciousness connects to the source field of divine creative energy from which all of material reality emerges. I believe it is this point we are looking for when we "search for God", a point that can only be found from within oneself, and once found, shines from us to be reflected back as the beauty of the world around us. I have a tendency to understand this point of *God* within us as the reflection of a grander reality. Our perceived individual lives are cross sections of *God* consciousness experiencing itself subjectively through interacting in a relativistic, consensus reality. The only thing preventing us from directly experiencing our complete *God self* at all times is the ego: the psychological mechanism that facilitates a perception of separateness, stores the *syntax* of cultural conditioning, and allows us to interact with each other and experience the relative wonders of life.

Psilocybin mushrooms have the potential to temporarily dissolve this ego function and facilitate the direct experience of *God*, a state of being that can arise from the total dissolution of the ego. Since the ego is responsible for the perception of separateness from our divine emotional creativity, or from *God*, we come closer to experiencing *oneness* with *All That Is, All At Once* when it is dissolved. Miester Eckhart, a Christian philosopher, described this experience as connecting to the 'Godhead'.

We can see these archetypal processes of accessing an awareness of *God* in other religious traditions as well. In Sufism, a mystical school of the Islamic tradition, it is stated those who love God are gifted three blessings: Islam (submission/surrender), Iman (faith) and Ishan (awareness of God[42]). Mushrooms can open our psychoemotional perception with such force that we may have no other choice but to give into its power (Islam) and have faith or trust in our *self* (Iman) that we will come through it alive. It is in this *surrender* and trust that we may get a glimpse of the true depth of *spirit* (Ishan).

The connection between psilocybin mushrooms and their potential to temporarily dissolve the functions of the ego and connect us to *spirit* is at least partially responsible for their ability to occasion mystical experiences. Applying this concept to other religious thought, unhindered by personal belief systems defining "what God is" and "what psilocybin mushrooms are not", we will find parallels of this idea across a wide spectrum of religious thought.

In discussing *God*, we have generally focused on the positive aspects of the mushroom experience. Many people seem to focus primarily on these pleasantries of psilocybin; however, this is only one part of a grander spectrum of potential outcomes. Often, the psilocybin experiences that facilitate this connection with *God* arise through the process of facing and dealing with a flood of severely uncomfortable emotions, sometimes misunderstood as "bad trips". It is through this uncomfortable process we can gain the most beneficial results of exploring the healing capacities of psilocybin.

EMOTIVE-PSYCHOSYNTHESIS

Psychospiritual growth is an energetic process of cyclical change. It is the development of cultivating psychospiritual maturity: a state where one is able to confidently and consciously embody expressions of their deeper *self*, unhindered by the unconscious self-repression generated through cultural conditioning. One aspect of psychospiritual growth is allowing inner-truth—expressions of the deeper *self*—to emerge through *surrendering* to the honest flow of emotion. This is called *emotive-psychosynthesis**.

Much like photosynthesis—a plant's process of converting the elements of their environment into the nutrients required for growth—*emotive-psychosynthesis* occurs when we allow for the latent energy of an emotion or emotional state to be processed and recycled back into the mental-emotional system. When we allow ourselves this *emotive-psychosynthesis* by letting emotions flow naturally, we fuel psychospiritual growth. But when we repress emotion, consciously or not, we retard psychospiritual growth. That emotional repression will become blockages in the body's energetic flow, and the longer these blockages remain unaddressed, the more difficult they become to release. Eventually, these blockages will manifest in the body/mind system as psychological and physical dis-ease. Through the practice of *surrender*, psilocybin helps to process a broad spectrum of these blockages by generating an experience of emotional intensity potent enough to dissolve them. Unfortunately, when psilocybin-facilitated *emotive-psychosynthesis* is misunderstood as a "bad trip", *surrender* is resisted, and the potential benefits of that experience are arrested.

All life is a cyclical process of energetic change. For example, at a biochemical level, the elements required for life to grow are metabolized

---

* 'Psychosynthesis' is a term originally introduced by psychologist Roberto Assagioli. According to Assagioli, we have a variety of different sub-personalities operating deep within the psyche at any given time, which rise to the surface in relation to specific contexts. He described 'psychosynthesis' as a process of recognizing these sub-personalities and integrating them into a holistic sense of *self*.

and broken down by microorganisms into their base components. Those base components are then recycled to create and nourish life in other organisms. A plant, for example, sustains life through photosynthesis—wherein it takes carbon dioxide, water, and light to create glucose, its food source, while also converting that carbon dioxide into oxygen. The oxygen is then used by animals, including us, to facilitate a variety of biological functions needed to live. An animal's respiration results in the conversion of that oxygen back into carbon dioxide, which the plants then use for photosynthesis again. Animals also eat plants, break them down into smaller nutrients through digestion and excrete their waste back onto the ground. This waste contains nutrients that filter down to fertilize soil and nourish other plants to grow, thus perpetuating the cycle. This exchanging of essential elements for life is happening all the time, through a huge variety of different cycles, which all interrelate with each other. This is the circle of life.

Emotions are manifestations of life-force energy. They are the surface-level experience of different expressions of this energy, unique to each individual. *Emotive-psychosynthesis* is the process of metabolizing the unfolding energy of these emotional manifestations by allowing ourselves to feel those emotions with an honest expression. This is not to imply that we release self-control and allow emotion to dictate our actions, rather, that we *surrender* ourselves to fully experience those emotions without hindering, projecting, or hiding from them. This *surrender* results in the benefit of preventing energetic blockages and thus, mitigating the negative consequences caused by emotional repression. There are lessons that arise about *self* and life from this process that help us to better navigate ourselves and generate psychospiritual maturity through self-awareness. In *emotive-psychosynthesis* we metabolize and break down the emotional manifestation of life-force energy back into a raw state, creating a fertilizer for psychospiritual growth.

Emotive-psychosynthesis is not an easy process to undergo, especially in the cultural conditioning of Western society. We are not given an effective *language* for allowing emotions to flow in honesty. Instead of learning tools to effectively navigate emotional experience, as children, we are taught to "calm down", "be quiet", and "control yourself". We grow up internally reiterating these words through a self-perpetuating *language* of repression. As adults now fully engrained with this self-repressing system, it becomes very difficult to *surrender* into the honest flow of emotion. Without a *language* to navigate beyond this self-repression, we will not have any relative perspective to gauge how deeply we are being held back by it. Mostly, we are given a *language* wherein the truth of emotional experience is hindered from being represented openly, and enforced by culturally conditioned *judgments* unfolding internally and socially. With *languages* such as office politics, all sadness being signs of illness, the fallacy of masculine emotional strength and feminine emotional hysteria, "don't cry in public", and "keep your problems to yourself," it is as if we are all expected to be business professional robots while in the public sphere. Even just these few examples are clear evidence of a cultural conditioning that supports a repugnant self-perpetuating system of repression and illness.

Because of an upbringing in this type of social environment, most of us live unconsciously avoiding, suppressing, or downright denying the truth of who we are and of our divine emotional creativity. Similar to the conditioned mind's impulsive inner-labeling process automatically pushing away anything that doesn't fit within its *syntax*, this culturally given *language* molds us into self-repressing business professional robots. Yet, each time we suppress, hide, or deny an emotion, its energetic flow is blocked. It is then stored undigested somewhere within the body—in our muscles, organs, joints etc. Our emotion's potential energy for facilitating psychospiritual growth and self-understanding is thus stunted. We end up slowing or even stopping psychospiritual growth because we have stopped allowing *emotive-psychosynthesis*. We have unconsciously cultivated an energetic dormancy that cuts off the necessary nutrients for psychospiritual growth, present within emotional energy.

Even without the *language* to be aware of this dormancy, it still has effect. Eventually the damned reservoirs of undigested emotions will begin to rupture. They may manifest as confusion about life, self-alienation, an inability to deal with minor changes, or other psychological and emotional hindrances. These manifestations will ultimately lead to deep levels of anxiety and stress, which gets offloaded onto the physical body, preventing its normal functioning and causing psychosomatic chronic inflammation.

There are a variety of methods available that may help to re-surface these undigested clumps of denied emotion. Almost all of them, however, require long, arduous efforts and a deep commitment to dissolving these blockages, which can be very difficult after years of patterned denial and repression. The longer we hold these blockages, the denser they become; the longer we hide from them, the scarier they will be. Out of a *fear* of emotional blockages, consciously or not, we hold ourselves back from investigating these emotions or allowing them to flow honestly. This *fear* can be so strong that it even unconsciously prevents us from releasing these blockages during a conscious attempt to do so. It can take a lot of work to develop the ability and confidence to *surrender* into such blockages.

What I believe as the core purpose of psychotherapy is to help people bring up these undigested emotions to be metabolized, enabling them to move on with their lives. Unfortunately, the longer we let these emotional blockages fester, the more difficult releasing these blockages will be. Often, people will spend years in conventional psychotherapy without much progress. In my opinion, the failure by established academics of Western psychotherapy to consider psychospiritual growth as an element of a person's state of health is the reason it can so be ineffective.

Anti-depressant SSRI (selective serotonin re-uptake inhibitor) drugs such as Prozac and Zoloft, address the mental illnesses associated to emotional repression by alleviating their symptoms. Due to how slowly they work and often unsuccessful they are, as well as the frequency in which they are prescribed, SSRI's may be one of the most dangerous forms of treatment currently in use[*]. They chemically generate a shallow emotional state of complacency by suppressing the hard feelings that are arising from the consequences of emotional repression. These chemicals

---

[*] This is my opinion. If you are currently taking SSRI's, please do not change or discontinue your regimen without consulting your healthcare professional as this is potentially dangerous and can be counter-productive to your healing.

may hide the symptoms of psychological illness and leave the cause untreated. They effectively shut off the ability to allow for emotional honesty and thus prevent addressing the root of those illnesses: stagnant emotional energy. There are therapeutic programs that utilize the effective suppression of negative feelings as an avenue to help with therapy, though people often still invest years ingesting these drugs on a daily basis, and getting almost nowhere. This long-term, ineffective treatment can end up costing thousands of dollars on drugs that are not helping people get well. The overzealous frequency of prescribing SSRI drugs might not be such a horrendous element of the Western medical system if we didn't already have the means address these psychoemotional illnesses effectively... but we do.

Psychedelics may do the opposite of SSRI's. Depending on the dose, environment, and intention for use, they can catalyze the surfacing of repressed emotions in full force, allowing for *emotive-psychosynthesis*. Psilocybin, in particular, can bring up these repressed emotional blockages and encourage addressing them in a manner that cannot be evaded. The process of *surrendering* to the honesty of our emotional experiences as it is occasioned by psilocybin, whether challenging or not, is greatly beneficial to healing the cause of many psychological dis-eases. It helps us bring up and dissolve deep-seated emotional blockages from within the psyche. This is a process I feel conventional clinical psychotherapy attempts to cultivate, often without success.

Psychotherapy's often slow and unsuccessful results are because patients usually have a strong psychological tendency to hold themselves back from consciously connecting with the emotional root of their illness. This is an autonomic defense mechanism intended to avoid suffering the discomfort of emotional responsibility. The therapist is attempting to circumvent this defense mechanism and stimulate the needed emotional release, as if trying to bypass a computer firewall. Psilocybin is more successful than conventional psychotherapy in bypassing these defense mechanisms because it works like a computer program that shuts down the firewall defenses altogether. This forces us to release from resisting honest emotions. From here, we are then able to *surrender* to emotional honesty and dissolve the emotional blockages. Instead of being agitated into an emotional release from the outside in, as is the case in conventional psychotherapy, with psilocybin, this process of releasing these defense mechanisms are easier because we are *surrendering* to a force arising from within, pushing its way out. We need only to allow it.

When exposed to an honest emotional experience through psilocybin, we are presented with an emotional potency beyond anything ever felt, especially if we have spent our lives in emotional suppression. When we let go of our defenses and face the reality of our emotional depths—whether pleasant or not—we open ourselves to *emotive-psychosynthesis,* to healing, and to the cultivation of psychospiritual maturity. It is *surrendering* to this emotional potency that facilitates the dissolution of emotional blockages. Through generating an energetic force that surpasses the density of these blockages, psilocybin offers us a way to transcend the cultural conditioning of emotional repression. It fuels the cycles of psychospiritual growth by stimulating the release of psychological defense mechanisms, and allowing the *emotive-psychosynthesis* of long repressed emotions. When we learn to *surrender* to the emotional honesty of a psilocybin experience and begin the metabolizing of repressed emotional issues, we change the emotional perspective by which we interact with *self* and the world. It helps to inspire us out of narrow-minded, culturally conditioned perspectives, and enables us to observe and interact with the world from a point of honesty, openness, and a holistic self-awareness—a point of clearer vision.

Facing the Shadow

A Deep-Seated Fear

As we go through the process of mental-emotional self-discovery and the psychospiritual growth that follows it, we often find ourselves repeating self-destructive habits. Making poor choices, mistakes, and following fruitless directions in life may be a necessary part of the psychospiritual growth process. Still, why is it that despite realizing that certain habitual choices are repeatedly bringing us to the same pitfalls, we continue those habits? Why is it that even with a desire to move efficiently along our journey through life, there is a sense that we are working against ourselves? Of course there is no single answer to this, as each person is unique in his or her challenges. But there is one archetypal challenge that plays a major role: *fear*.

Acute fear—the physiological response to a sense of danger; a powerful tool for survival—is not the type of fear I am referencing. In saying *fear*, I am specifically addressing *chronic fear*—an ongoing emotional state with no specific cause. *Chronic fear* operates in the background of our lives, seated in the substrate of awareness, constantly informing the experience of reality and adversely affecting the ability to make sound decisions. When strongly present, it debilitates us from making wise choices towards constructive psychospiritual growth. *Chronic fear* is among the greatest obstacles to growth within *self* and the human species.

As a physiological mechanism, the purpose of *acute fear* is to stimulate a response of survival stress—fight or flight—when confronted with danger. With *chronic fear* there is no specific danger, and so we stay in this state of stress continuously. This ongoing stress takes a toll on the body just like emotional repression, eventually leading to psychosomatic inflammation and illness. The emotional stress of *fear* puts us in a state where the body is unable to facilitate its regulatory processes at the cellular level. When a cell is properly facilitating its regulatory processes, like respiration and division, it is in a state of *growth*. When under the perception of danger, it enters into a state called *protection*. In *protection*, all metabolic processes in the cell are put on hold and the cell prepares itself for quick bursts of self-preserving action[43].

The sense of danger that causes the cellular body to enter *protection* does not need to be a legitimate danger present in physical reality. It can be caused by any perception of danger, even if it is a false perception. Being in a state of fear, founded on false perceptions, will cause cells to enter *protection* as much as being in real danger. This means that if we maintain consistent anxiety because of *chronic fear*, we eventually cause a breakdown of functioning in the body due to prolonged periods of time without *growth*. As previously stated, fear itself is a natural response. It is what helps us navigate dangers in the environment. But when fear is constructed on false perceptions, as is the case with *chronic fear*, it holds us back from personal growth. Not just psychospiritually, but physiologically as well, through the inhibiting of cellular *growth*.

The mentality informed by *chronic fear* perpetually generates the perception of obstacles in life by turning our decisions into reactions against anything that may bring awareness to this ongoing *fear*. Lacking a *language* to navigate this *fear*, we end up retreating from that which roused this awareness. Receding into the comfort of emotional familiarity, where we experience the least potential *fear*, even if that familiarity is an emotional state wherein we are uncomfortable and repeat self-destructive patterns. This recession into emotional familiarity slows or even prevents psychospiritual growth, as what we need for this growth are choices in life made on the basis of moving towards something desirable (i.e., happiness), not just moving away from something feared.

In order to redirect focus from fear-based reactions to self-confident, courageous, and constructive personal growth, we must address and dissolve *chronic fear*. We do this by first recognizing that a major cause of *chronic fear* is directly facing our fears: the fears of dealing with responsibilities, of dealing with the past, dealing with debt, with relationships, with lies, the fears of dealing with the honesty of our emotional experiences, etc. We generate *chronic fear* by evading the experiential weight of the emotional potency for fear itself and all of its associations in life. Once we learn to face the root—the emotional potential for the experience of fear—we will learn how to differentiate between *acute fear* rising from legitimate danger and *chronic fear*, founded on false-perceptions and cultural conditioning. This enables us to become mindful of and move beyond the obstacles of *chronic fear*. This is not an easy task.

Often, we are not offered opportunities during the early years of development to learn how to face our deep fears, as it is not a part of our cultural traditions. We lack the once-unanimous practice of rituals that cultivated this type of experience for discovering and exploring courage. We thus lack the *language* in our cultural *syntax* for finding a personal sense of inner-strength, standing confidently in the face of fear, and unlocking an ability to live with a true sense of inner-freedom. Instead, cultural conditioning has trained us to desperately avoid facing fear at all, while simultaneously embedding *languages* that re-enforce *chronic fear*.

I see us brought up in a society that encourages cultivating a perception of happiness and comfort, contentment and solace, passivity and compliance through social norms that label any uncomfortable or dark emotional experience as sick or wrong—effectively removing us from recognizing the benefit of discomfort and challenge. This disconnects us from recognizing our fullest personal capability to deal with fear, change, and challenge. All the while, in order to maintain the cultural status quo of political and social hierarchical control, this same society perpetuates *chronic fear* through various modes of manipulation, such as mass media propaganda force-feeding its participants a reality of rampant consumerism, economic scarcity, and self-repression. In participating with this societal norm, we perpetuate a *language* that encourages *chronic fear* and the evasion of emotional responsibility, a *language* deficient in genuine self-confidence, mutual respect, compassion, or courage. This dynamic confluence of manipulating forces keeps us unconscious to the dramatic presence of *chronic fear* and our full emotional potency.

Chronic fear is among life's greatest challenges and many of us lack the *syntax* to be aware of its detrimental effects. An ongoing unfamiliarity in facing fear gives rise to anxiety and the avoidance of anything that may stimulate uncomfortable emotional experiences. This occasions all sorts of unconsciously compulsive, irrational, and self-limiting behaviors. When we lock our doors and don't go out after dark, chances are, we are not hiding from the identifiable object of *acute fear*. We are hiding from the external projections of internal *chronic fear*. We do so because most of us have not experienced the honest emotional potency of fear itself. As a result, we lack the sense of inner-strength that reveals our capability of great courage. In order to awaken to this fuller potential as human beings, to truly develop psychospiritual maturity, we must first address the thing that hold us back: the root of *chronic fear,* our darkness, the *shadow*. If we do not face these elements of *self,* we will not truly mature but instead, project a false persona.

When unaddressed, this darkness is hidden until it is agitated. It then flares out upon whatever inflamed it, be that ourselves or another person. This means we must face and overcome *chronic fear,* elsewise others will end up bearing the weight of its burden. To dissolve *chronic fear's* hindrances, we must learn how to recognize, address, and overcome it as it presents itself. Paradoxically, it is impossible to eliminate fear completely, nor would we want to, as it can be a tool for survival and the means by which we can discover great courage.

> *Acknowledging fear is not cause for depression or discouragement. Because we posses such fear, we are also potentially entitled to experience fearlessness. True Fearlessness is not the reduction of fear, but the going beyond fear.*
>
> *- Chögyam Trungpa*[44]

In order to learn a new skill, such as learning to go beyond fear or how to address fear in daily life, we need practice. Something small that will allow us to transfer the lessons learned from this small practice to a broader spectrum. These practices do not intend to reduce or eliminate fear, but work to reduce the amount of things we are afraid of and the debilitating effects of fear. Consequently, they would also help us to reduce anxiety and stress in daily life.

We could learn the skill of going beyond fear through a variety of methods. Meditation is the foundation of all of them, the end and beginning of all lasting self-development. Meditation in its simplest form—wherein we simply sit and bear witness to thoughts and feelings from a non-attached, non-involved perspective—allows us to learn how to address the surface level manifestations of our deep-seated fears and emotional repression, without allowing those manifestations to take control. This approach allows us the ability to leverage ourselves into a space of acceptance and relaxation, which when applied outwardly onto daily life, enables psychospiritual growth even in the midst of a fear response.

Another important method of processing and addressing the root of fear is to go directly into that fear, experiencing a full catharsis, until we can tell which type of fear is bred of survival (*acute fear*) and which type of fear is bred of culturally conditioned evasion (*chronic fear*). Working with a practice that generates a potent cathartic experience will help do two things: it will provide proof by personal experience that we possess the capability of dealing with the things in life that we are afraid of, and over time, will make us more aware of which fears we hold within and help us learn to overcome them. But be careful, darkness is a hard place to be in, especially if you are there alone.

Since the false presumptions of *chronic fear* encourage emotional repression, they are a major hindrance to personal growth and resist the natural *synchronistic flow of life* found through *surrender*. In the same way psilocybin helps dissolve emotional repression through *emotive-psychosynthesis*, it can help in reducing *chronic fear* by revealing great courage through the process of *facing the shadow*. In learning how to face the root of fear, to face the *shadow*, we also begin to reduce the emotional resistance to the unfolding events of life. We begin to reduce the chronic inflammation associated with emotional repression and fear. We ultimately develop confidence within an ability to deal with whatever life brings, allowing us release into its *synchronistic flow* and enjoy the ride.

> *Don't try to push the river; it flows by itself.*
> *-Anonymous*

THE SHADOW

The *shadow* was first introduced by psychiatrist Carl Gustav Jung. As a part of his model of the human subconscious, the *shadow* is the personification of all the aspects of *self* that we avoid facing; all the aspects of *self* we choose to not deal with consciously[45]. He felt that if the *shadow* is not addressed and integrated into a conscious understanding of *self*, it would become darker, denser, and we would not be able to become *whole.*[46] This concept of the *shadow* has evolved since Jung presented it, and a variety of different perspectives on it, and its functional role, have since been presented.

As I have come to understand it, the *shadow* is one's potential for dark emotional experiences—i.e., fear, anger, sadness, regret, selfishness, guilt, shame, etc. It refers to the amalgamation of all dark emotions. Many theories focus on one's dark personality traits as being the *shadow*. I believe, however, the *shadow* is actually the emotional root associated to these traits, which are only a surface level manifestation of the *shadow*. They are unconscious reactions to the emotional potential for darkness that lay within, played out in accordance to the conditioning of the ego.

The surface level aspects of the *shadow* we can observe and relate to—i.e., personality traits such as a tendency to unconsciously manipulate others—are only the branches and leaves. It is in the depths of the emotional being that we find the roots of this darkness. In these depths we find the origins of *chronic fear* and the cultivation of psychospiritual maturity. Jung felt as though we cannot become *whole* if we do not understand and integrate the *shadow*. I feel this is because until we face the emotional darkness within, we will continue to play out unconscious conditioned patterns in order to avoid *facing the shadow*. We cannot become *whole* if there are elements of ourselves we evade. The result of this evasion is further emotional repression and the negative aspects of life associated with repression, such as dark personality traits portrayed through the conditioned reactions of the ego.

Facing the shadow is as important to psychospiritual growth as allowing for the *emotive-psychosynthesis* of repressed emotions and overcoming *chronic fear*. But the challenge of *facing the shadow* is a great one. It is the expression of all that we fear most within ourselves. Many are reluctant to even consider addressing this challenge. Instead, the reaction is to only focus on the light aspects of life, of "living in the love dimension". It is important not to get weighted by the darkness of life, but to avoid responsibility for its presence is as destructive to psychospiritual maturation as wallowing in self-deprecation and *judgment*.

I feel many people choose to focus on this light rather than addressing the truth of their own darkness for two major reasons. The first is that the darkness inside of us is powerful and the longer we have avoided facing it, the darker and denser it becomes. Consequently, it becomes easier to center on the light than face the challenge of *emotive-psychosynthesis* and *facing the shadow*. The second is that we lack the personal experience of knowing we can face this darkness and so we do not see our courage. Both of these reasons are expressions of *chronic fear,* and later, we will discuss how they can be addressed through conscious work with psilocybin mushrooms.

Until we face the *shadow*, address the truth of darkness, and become aware of how this darkness is playing out in our lives, we will condemn ourselves to being creatures of impulsive evasion, repression, and reactivity. These impulses will work against psychospiritual growth and negatively affect the people around us—as is the case in *manifested judgment*, which is an obvious expression of evaded darkness—but one people may not fully understand.

MANIFESTED JUDGEMENT

Whether it is understood or recognized by the conscious mind, all that we perceive as outside ourselves is painted with an emotional significance—a *meaningfulness*—generated within and projected outwards onto the world. This means everything we perceive as outside of ourselves is a reflection of what is within. When we are afraid of the *shadow*, its presence is repressed and avoided, and we will likely generate *chronic fear*. That *fear* will then become the *meaningfulness* projected onto the outside world. We then perceive this false self-generated projection as a *meaningfulness* of "danger" from outside ourselves and react accordingly. It is not a real danger but a deeper, feared aspect of our *self* being projected upon the perceivably external elements of life and reacted to as if it were real. We paint a *meaningfulness* of *chronic fear* upon otherwise ordinary occurrences.

Chronic fear arises from lacking awareness of both the light and dark aspects of *self* and a reluctance to take responsibility for addressing the potential to directly experience darkness, or the *shadow*. This evasion influences us to unconsciously externalize this *fear* by projecting it outwards onto the external environment. Projected *fear* works as a *languaging* structure that clouds decision-making and hinders the ability to see the things in our environment that may actually be dangerous and warrant *acute fear*.

If we fear dealing with the dark aspects of *self*, choosing to ignore their existence, repressing and projecting them, they will continue to hinder psychospiritual maturity. Consciously or not, these choices negatively affect not only our personal lives, but the lives of those around us as well. Hidden from the light of awareness, the repressed *shadow* will eventually show its face and manifest as subtleties in how we interact with the world around us. One of the subtle manifestations of this repression is called *manifested judgment*.

Personal choices of actions, thoughts, and feelings are always associated in some way to the emotional root of the *shadow*, thus play a strong role in directing the expression of personality. This means the emotional discomfort associated with undesired elements of personality can work like signposts to direct us towards the *shadow*. Knowing this enables the self-awareness of emotional discomfort, to be used as a means to face the *shadow* and enable *emotive-psychosynthesis*. However, if we choose to avoid taking responsibility in addressing the emotions associated with undesired personality traits and repress them instead, those signposts to the *shadow* begin to point outwards onto the people around us. We hold *judgment* against others for certain aspects of their personality because they expose to us the same aspects of ourselves that we have chosen to deny. We then emotionally react against others for the aspects of *self* we avoided responsibility for as if it were their fault. This is *manifested judgment*. When the undesired personality traits we have chosen to avoid responsibility for are reflected back at us, we emotionally react according to personal discomfort. The fault of this discomfort is projected outwards onto others in the form of *judgment*. It does not always manifest as comparative value statements, like, "uh, what a fatso!" Often, *judgment* is expressed simply by interacting with others from the relative perspective of an unprocessed emotional reaction, in order to avoid dealing with the content of conditioned repression.

Almost all of us are brought up with a *syntax* that promotes immediate *judgment* of others; it is a part of cultural conditioning. Yet essentially, we are only *judging* ourselves and projecting it onto one another to make it easier to deal with. When *judging* others, as a vast majority of us do, we are effectually living a lie for which others suffer. Unfortunately, many do not yet recognize this lie and may never want to. But if we want to develop psychospiritual maturity and become *whole,* it is our responsibility to address this *language* of *judgment* and alleviate others from suffering the negative emotional baggage of the personal *shadow* being projected onto them. If we do not choose to accept this responsibility, we will continue to emotionally offload the burden of personal darkness onto others, most often, onto those we love.

The only source of *judgment* exists within. When we accept that *judgment* is based on a resistance to accepting ourselves, we are able to release others from the fault and responsibility of our personal issues.

> *Do not judge, or you too will be judged. For in the same way you judge others, you will be judged, and with the measure you use, it will be measured to you. Why do you look at the speck of sawdust in your brother's eye and pay no attention to the plank in your own eye? How can you say to your brother, 'Let me take the speck out of your eye,' when all the time there is a plank in your own eye? You hypocrite, first take the plank out of your own eye, and then you will see clearly to remove the speck from your brother's eye.*
>
> *Mathew 7:1-5 (New International Version)*[47]

Like learning to deal with fear, in order to address and integrate the *shadow* aspects of *self,* we should seek to find a practice that can bring us face to 'face with them. When we open up to *facing the shadow* through accepting responsibility for undesired personal traits, we allow for an *emotive-psychosynthesis* of their associated emotional discomfort, thus nourishing psychospiritual maturation. Generally, psychotherapy is an attempt to poke and prod manifestations of the *shadow* to bring about an honest emotional reaction. But this method attempts to work backwards by first finding the associated manifestations of the *shadow* and agitating them to track down its emotional root. There are more effective ways to face the *shadow* and cultivate psychospiritual growth.

The practice of meditation, which I personally consider very important for anybody on a conscious path of psychospiritual maturation, is a way to allow for *emotive-psychosynthesis* without active agitation. Specifically, a type of meditation practice where we sit and cultivate a non-*judgmental* awareness of passing thoughts. This exposes us to what is happening beneath the surface of the mind while we sit in a state of active non-identification with what arises. A meditation practice like this allows us to integrate the content arising from within as present and real, with an honest emotional awareness, and without immediately assigning fault for those emotions. This practice is very important in developing the necessary *language* for navigating the *shadow* effectively and thus dissolving *judgmental* projections against others.

The evasion of accepting responsibility for addressing the *shadow* through repression and projection runs deep within us. If we are to come to a full awareness of how much projection we are facilitating, we must enter those depths. This means we choose to bring about a potent emotional awareness of the repressed *self,* which allows the associated manifestations of those aspects to shine into conscious observation. Psilocybin mushrooms can help facilitate that. Like combining the intention of psychotherapy and the process of meditation together, mushrooms bring the most prevalent emotional repression within us to the surface of awareness. We can then take responsibility for the emotional energy of this repression by *surrendering* to it. This process relieves the ineffectiveness of trying to bring about *emotive-psychosynthesis* through hunting down the roots of the *shadow* by agitating its manifestations; instead, it takes us deep into the root and allows *emotive-psychosynthesis* to arise organically. This organic *emotive-psychosynthesis* can help to amplify psychospiritual maturation while avoiding external *languaging* structures that antagonize the *shadow*.

Even as we mature, the process of *judgment* and projection will continue. However, once we consciously choose to accept the responsibility of addressing undesired personality traits—through whatever method—we can begin to let go of our *judgment* of others, thus alleviating them of the emotional burden that goes with it. By accepting ourselves as fallible beings with a potential for great darkness, taking responsibility for emotional discomfort, and investigating the *shadow* with an earnest and unbiased observation, we open up to understanding that we are dealing with negative aspects within ourselves through the *manifested judgment* of others. We open up to the understanding that to *judge* or ostracize others for these traits is really to *judge* or ostracize ourselves. From here we can begin to develop a *language* that navigates the conditioning of *judgment* as constructive signposts towards the *shadow,* rather than negative projections against others. Our relationships, specifically with the ones we tend to project against the most—our loved ones—can then become a mutual practice of cultivating psychospiritual maturity in each other through communication, responsibility, and compassion.

PSILOCYBIN AND THE SHADOW

Psilocybin mushrooms guide us into a state of increased emotional awareness, and in doing so, are able to bring us into a direct encounter with the *shadow*. When used with maturity and respect, they can help us to address enduring psychospiritual blockages. During these encounters with the *shadow,* the mushrooms can guide us into the emotional roots of *self* where the hard truth of psychoemotional wounds can be faced directly, released, and healed. Yet, when used out of ignorance, *shadow* experiences with psilocybin may further emotional repression and worsen the consequential blockages. The results of *facing the shadow* depend entirely on how we choose to interact with it.

While *facing the shadow*—immersed in the potent emotional environment psilocybin unlocks—we are offered new perspectives on how the *shadow* manifests in our lives, and powerful lessons about the *shadow* aspects of *self* in general. These lessons and perspectives are generally communicated in two ways. First, through a direct visitation of *shadow*-inspired choices—i.e., actions, thoughts, or feelings from the past (or potential choices in the future) associated with uncomfortable or repressed emotions; and second, through creative ideas or metaphors founded on personally relevant symbolism—i.e., a strange and novel, yet deeply personal visionary experience, wherein the underlying emotional concept is directly relevant to repression.

When we understand we are *facing the shadow* and choose to *surrender*, these experiences enable a powerful opportunity for cultivating self-awareness, personal growth, and healing. However, if we do not understand the breadth of what is happening to us, we may create resistance, anxiety, and further emotional repression and projection—as is often the case with young recreational users.

Many people begin taking psilocybin recreationally with the intention of playfulness and without understanding its potential to expose the uncomfortable honesty of the *shadow*. Regardless of intention, as one continues to explore the emotional depths of *self* with this substance, a tendency to journey deeper and deeper with each session may occur, and eventually, this light-heartedness may be challenged. Occasions arise where recreational intentions and a lack of understanding result in poor choices regarding the decision to indulge, and one may end up forced into addressing the darkness that lays within. This unexpected and unrequested experience can be very challenging and uncomfortable. It is that first hard experience, the "bad trip", which generally stops recreational users from exploring the substance further. Due to a lack of understanding and an abundance of stigma, many people in the position of having had that experience end up blaming the mushrooms for being "bad" or the "drug" not being "right" for them. Yet, the problem was not the substance; rather, the user was not prepared to handle the dark emotional honesty exposed during that experience. In this type of circumstance, the emotional flow is resisted, *surrender* and *emotive-psychosynthesis* denied, and all the possible benefits of *facing the shadow* are discarded. The potential lessons of that dark experience are rejected, and the substance is blamed to avoid dealing with the challenge of owning personal responsibility for being the source of that experience. It is true that psilocybin mushrooms are not for everybody, but this is because not everybody is prepared to deal with the intensity of emotional honesty exposed during the experience*.

The rush that comes with psilocybin is one of extreme emotional energy. It cannot be stopped; it can only be *surrendered* to or futilely resisted. A direct experience of the *shadow* is very challenging, but addressing the things that arise within it can expose us to a broader self-awareness and understanding of life. By *surrendering* into the dark emotions exposed during *shadow* experiences, we have the rare opportunity to look with humbled eyes into the uncomfortable truth of emotional repression and allow *emotive-psychosynthesis* to take place. This provides us a vantage point to see life beyond the psychoemotional weight of self-repression, denial, and cultural conditioning.

The *shadow* is where our most challenging experiences come from, and to enter the source of those experiences catalyzes an intensity of emotion that cannot be understood until we are there. In the midst of this challenge, the mushroom can work like a *guide*. It can direct the light of awareness towards personal landmarks in the mind, in a way that enables us to better navigate the darkness. These landmarks are where we store bravery, courage, self-confidence, strength, compassion, etc. Thus, in this experience of exploring the darkness with mushrooms, we are gifted reminders of the light. The moments of facing my darkness with psilocybin mushrooms have been among the most difficult experiences of my life, but they have given me a beautiful sense of confidence and courage in facing life's everyday challenges.

Psilocybin brings the dark aspects of the emotional *self* to the surface of awareness with full intensity. When in this space, the conscious mind begins to expose us to the life experiences associated with these dark aspects, which are the surface-level manifestations of our emotional repression and potential for darkness. The psilocybin mushroom exposes

---

* Excluding people with current, or a family history of, severe mental illness, which can be potentiated through psychedelic use. These people should be very cautious in their choice of using psychedelics.

the surface of personal hardships by bringing us into the depths of their origin, but it does more than just take us there. It helps us process these hardships and bring a conscious understanding of how to navigate them. As we learn to work with psilocybin and develop the ability to *surrender* into the emotional honesty it potentiates, we become more capable of metabolizing the repressed emotions it exposes. We learn confidence in allowing *emotive-psychosynthesis,* and gain an ability to navigate and integrate challenging emotional experiences as a process of healing and maturation in all areas of life. The mushroom helps us to metabolize the potential energy contained within challenging emotional experiences and direct it towards psychospiritual maturation.

Fungi are the decomposers of our planet. Without their role in death and decay there would be no life. Psilocybin, like all fungus, plays this role as well. By guiding us into the *emotive-psychosynthesis* of emotional repression, it *decomposes the shadow* and unlocks the nutrients contained within it to feed the soil of psychospiritual growth. They take us on a journey through and beyond the death and decay of repression, into the fertile grounds of budding maturity, courage, and confidence.

Through breaking down the emotional blockages that hinder us, the psilocybin experience guides us through the *shadow* and beyond, into the empowerment of personal responsibility and psychospiritual maturity. It helps us learn the ability to *surrender* ourselves into the honesty of dark emotional experiences without projection, assures us we are ready and capable of going further, and enables us see the true strength residing within the release of personal blockages. It exposes us to the crucial understanding that the *shadow* can be among our greatest spiritual tools once we learn to navigate it. If founded on respect and the intention of healing, a practice with the psilocybin mushroom can bring about a full and successful integration of a fragmented emotional existence into an expression of *whole self.*

Choosing to explore psilocybin with conscious intent opens the door to a caliber of experience that once opened, cannot be closed again. It's like learning a new language. If we learn French, for example, we will not be able to stop the mind from interpreting the French language when it is heard. The same goes for the psilocybin experience. Once these experiences become dark, we may be forced to face an even deeper darkness each time we re-enter the psilocybin space. When recognizing this potential and still choosing to work with the mushroom, this practice can become the experiential point of reference by which we explore and understand the deep courage residing within us.

RE-ENTRY

Recognizing the mushroom's capacity for occasioning intense emotional catharsis is a powerful milestone of one's practice of using it for psychospiritual maturation and the cultivation of personal courage. It can be difficult for someone to understand abstractly or hypothetically what might be experienced when *facing the shadow* with psilocybin if they have never experienced it. In that context, it already requires a strong courage to take psilocybin and face this unknown. It becomes even more challenging after one has already entered this darkness and gone through the harshest experience one could possibly imagine going through, to actively choose to do it again. It is in this context one begins to attune to a deep, primordial courage and express a full commitment to personal healing.

When we consciously choose to re-enter the psilocybin space after *facing the shadow*, we are choosing to face a fear whose true power has already been felt. Metaphorically speaking, if "fire" is the pain of *facing the shadow* and "demons" are personifications of repressed negative emotions and thought patterns within the *shadow,* then we develop the ability to step into the fire knowing the demons that lay forth. We are standing strong with the confidence we are able to face anything that may confront us within this honest darkness. This personal confidence and courage is an experiential marking-point of having nourished our psychospiritual soil, though this is not all we are offered in exchange for our efforts. After facing the demons within us—negative thought patterns, emotional repression, self-deprecating narratives, etc.—we are given the brief opportunity to see the world unhindered by them. We are inspired to see the world around us with a *language* of courage, wonder, and divinity.

The ability to stand with courage in the face of great personal challenge transfers into everyday life with a broad spectrum of applicability. For example, after spending hours alone in the *shadow* processing a full catharsis of the emotional potential for failure, the challenge of the first day at a new job isn't nearly as difficult to face. The sense of courage cultivated in facing the demons of one's mind far surpasses that which is needed to face the ordinary challenges of life. When learning to apply the lessons of *facing the shadow* into daily life, the trivial challenges that once inspired *chronic fear* hold little weight compared to the courage to face those challenges.

AFTER THE DARKNESS

In using psilocybin to enter emotional depths and face the manifestations of repression, fear, sorrow, loneliness, regret, etc., we face a challenge unlike any other. It is infinitely personal and unique; a challenge most other people will never confront with such intensity. It is very heavy, but through facing the darkness of *self* with *surrender* and courage, we are given the opportunity to experience something profoundly beautiful: a transcendent moment, *oneness*.

Facing the shadow and *surrendering* into *emotive-psychosynthesis* allows one's darkness to be released from repression: directly experienced and metabolized, decomposed. The emotional potency of the psilocybin mushroom guiding this experience enables large portions of repression to be integrated in relatively short periods of time compared to that of other spiritual practices and conventional psychotherapy. Emerging from a full exchange with the *shadow* through psilocybin, if we have completely *surrendered*, we are relieved of the despondent density of emotional repression. From this dark psychedelic process, there is a sense of lightness left over that becomes a point of reference for the interpretation of reality.

We are gifted a moment of *oneness*, of relief from a normally heavy existence into a lighter, wider awareness of life. This moment does not last very long and its benefit is defined entirely by how we choose to make use of it.

Having faced all the darkness we needed to at that moment in life—defined by the mysterious marriage of the mushroom and the subconscious—we are left with an abundance of the life-force energy that fuels psychospiritual growth. Previously stalled in the form of emotional repression and energetic blockages, it has now been released and is freely available to harness. After dissolving cultural conditioning and *decomposing the shadow* though an amplified *emotive-psychosynthesis*, our spiritual soil is nourished and ready to germinate fresh perspectives on *self* and life.

Still under the influence of psilocybin and only just awakening from the distinct clouding of hard times, we are fresh like newborns and can look upon the world without the limitations of a conditioned mind—where each element within our environment is automatically *languaged* and given a *meaningfulness* defined by culturally predetermined values. This moment is important, because it is one where we are able to take in beneficial perspectives to replace the negative conditioning and emotional repression we have just released. In this fresh space we are able to look upon the normal world free, for a moment, from the conceptual chains of the culturally conditioned mind. We can see the elements that construct the world with an increased psychological, emotional, and spiritual *meaningfulness*; we can see the world in a magical way with an ability to take in more beauty and wonder than previously possible. We are like a child who looks upon the majesty of a sunset for the first time and is awestruck by its glory. The difference between this experience and that of a child's is that within this innocent view of natural beauty, we still possess the developed intellect of a mature being. We are able to contemplate the powerful *meaningfulness* of this experience more so than possible as a child, or as an adult still locked into their conditioning. With a mature intelligence, we are able to contemplate the magnitude of what is happening to us. It is here that we are able to reset the *syntax* from the painful confrontation with *shadow* by inoculating it with a *language* that opens us to the full beauty of life.

After returning from the *oneness* experience, back to a normal waking state of consciousness, we can choose to contemplate, rationalize, and integrate the *language* we developed and the lessons that came with it. If we allow the emotional perspectives of *self* and the world to be illuminated by the interaction with a *meaningfulness* of transcendence and become a point of reference by which we observe reality, we change the world we live in from the inside out. By allowing the *language* of transcendence, learned through taking responsibility for our darkness to become the foundation of our identity, we begin to build a sense of *self* on the magic of personal dreams and visions—instead of a set of culturally conditioned values that do not necessarily serve us.

There are no guarantees with psilocybin, and the characteristics of a psilocybin experience can vary widely. Sometimes we may move into a state of *oneness* regardless of whether or not we have gone through a process of *facing the shadow*; other times we face the *shadow* and do not emerge into a state of *oneness*. That is the ambiguous nature of the mushroom experience. Still, there is one thing for sure: the experiential reward of *oneness* that can be learned through *facing the shadow* can never be obtained through avoiding it or evading responsibility for personal darkness.

ONENESS, MEANINGFULNESS, AND HEALING

Oneness is a state of being where we feel intimately connected to everything, to *All That Is, All At Once*. We may become overwhelmed by an encompassing sense of being loved, being love, and an unconditional gratitude for everything within the experience. Once we enter this state, the conscious mind begins to generate a series of ideas, memories, and a cascade of all sorts of benevolent feelings. The most encompassing expression of this beautiful experience is often referred to as a mystical experience, connection with the cosmos, or communion with God. It is an experience where the point of consciousness within us that connects with the *All That Is, All At Once* becomes the relative point of perspective by which we interpret reality.

As beings whose self-awareness is founded on a conceptual separation between "I" (observer) and "Not-I" (observed), we often attribute experiences that transcend the normal state of awareness as being separate from us. This tendency towards separateness may influence us to return from a psilocybin *oneness* experience with the misunderstanding that what we perceived was an external force. It is not an external force, but an internal experience. It is not the mushroom, it is not an externalized 'God' character. It is us. It is the perception of an internal force projected upon the environment and perceived as foreign due to unfamiliarity.

Similar to the manner in which we project *manifested judgment* onto others, we are constantly projecting internally generated *meaningfulness* onto the world. Everything we perceive as outside of us is a reflection of what is within us. This is to say that *syntax* doesn't just inform the manner in which we interact with the world; it is what informs the internal construction of reality itself. At its foundation, all life is simply patterns of energy and information. The reality we perceive is a projected interpretation of that information, and how that information is interpreted depends on the *syntax*. When we take in stimuli or data from the outside world, it is initially without any inherent *meaningfulness*. Once received, this data goes through the process of being subconsciously referenced to the inner-encyclopedia of experience and knowledge, or *syntax*. It then takes on psychological and emotional *meaningfulness*. This newly established m*eaningfulness* is then projected back outwards onto that which we perceive as external. Through a type of perceptual feedback loop, we subjectively create *meaningfulness* out of meaningless information and interact with that *meaningfulness* as if it were objectively real.

Consequently, the perception of a glorious and divinely beautiful world, one of prosperity and purpose, is sourced from within, as is the perception of a cold, dark and difficult world. When we come to the point in a psilocybin journey where we begin to see the outside world as transcending its previously materialistic, conditioned roles and into an open expression of enlightened life-force, it is a perspective that is sourced within us. To paraphrase the psychedelic alchemist Sasha Shulgin: the experience we have when we take substances is not the substances themselves but a portion of the mind's potential unlocked by the molecular key of those particular substances. When we enter the moment of mystical consciousness unlocked by psilocybin, the perception of a divine significance emanating from all things is an expression of the *self*. The psilocybin has simply allowed us to recognize our capacity to embody it, which can have profound healing effects.

Different psychoemotional states of being are different expressions of consciousness, each with a unique energetic pattern. When consciousness is expressed as *oneness*—divine, benevolent, love, etc.—the energy of that divine perception flows through us with positive effects on the mind and the body. Like the blessings of relief that can come from a laugh, this feeling of mystical transcendence or spiritual relation to the world around us can be very healing. It provides us transcendence from the weighted conditioning of daily life. It shows us what the world can be like when we are no longer clouded by the hindrances of the deep emotional trauma we may have. This can activate different psychological and physiological mechanisms that facilitate a broad spectrum of healing functions, even if that healing only lasts for a brief moment.

CULTIVATING PSYCHOSPIRITUAL MATURATION WITH PSILOCYBIN

When we learn to *surrender* to the emotional honesty of *oneness* in the same way we learn to *surrender* to the *shadow*, we start to develop a broad sense of self-awareness. Being able to look upon oneself with an understanding of both the extremely dark and light elements within, is an incredibly valuable tool for cultivating psychospiritual maturation. With self-awareness we are able to navigate the chaotic world around us without reacting to it according to the limitations of a conditioned *syntax*.

As we grow and experience life, we naturally develop self-awareness and psychospiritual maturation. However, the rate at which we cultivate self-awareness may be less than the rate at which we generate emotional repression and psychoemotional wounds. Depending on *syntax*, we may even slow psychospiritual maturation to a halt. This is why it becomes important for us to consciously cultivate self-awareness through some type of practice like meditation or psilocybin *ceremony*. If we choose to consciously interact with and learn about ourselves like we would a friend, we can balance the scales of healing in our favor, amplifying the rate of maturation. We can unwind cultural conditioning, release repression, and allow ourselves to consciously act from a place of self-awareness, rather than compulsively react based on cultural values and repressed psychoemotional wounds.

Unfortunately it seems as though we, as a species, learn better from hard times than we do when things are easy. Sometimes we are able to completely transcend pain and find healing without hurting, though often the cultivation of self-awareness comes from facing great emotional challenge, from *facing the shadow*. In knowing this, we are able to consciously face personal darkness and *surrender* into the honesty of its emotional experience, with a conscious understanding that in doing so we can dissolve repression, discover courage, and cultivate an expanded awareness of *self*.

There are many practices available to help us with psychospiritual maturation and healing past wounds; there are many paths along the way to the same destination. No single practice is right for everybody and you must find the path that is most harmonious for you. For me, psilocybin mushrooms have been a powerful choice and I feel very grateful for the lessons learned. They offered me the opportunity to investigate the emotional source of my choices in life and enabled the healing of past wounds through a deeply personal and incredibly challenging series of experiences.

When I chose to enter my relationship with the mushroom, I lacked a grounded reference in how to navigate the experience effectively. At first, I spent a lot of time emotionally stumbling, losing track of myself, and learning mostly through trial and error. Over time, I refined my practice and developed a *language* to navigate my experiences, integrate their *meaningfulness*, and share what I had learned. This *language* has enabled me to work with the mushroom effectively and better incorporate my experiences into daily life.

The mushroom can be a powerful tool, yet its benefits have been lost in a shroud of stigma, trivialization, recreational use, and rigid cultural belief systems. This powerful experience can be very foreign at first and there hasn't been a lot of grounded reference in the modern world for those who choose to investigate its potential. I believe the creation of a fresh *language* for navigating the novel characteristics of the psilocybin experience is vital at this time. This *language* can be like a map to reference in a foreign land; with it we are able to utilize the full potential of this medicine for personal healing, self-awareness, and psychospiritual maturation. These lessons translate into daily life and can inspire others.

Through *surrendering* to the emotional honesty of the psilocybin experience, whether it is in *oneness* or *facing the shadow*, we are able to re-pattern ourselves away from negative cultural conditioning. We can become aware of which aspects of *syntax* are fallacious, destructive, and unnecessary. We can learn to integrate the divine vision of the world that psilocybin unlocks, into a vision of *self* as well. Guided by the mushrooms, we can learn to dissolve the tendencies of self-depreciation, for at least a moment, and allow ourselves to be overwhelmed by self-appreciation and for the beauty all around us. We can use this medicine intentionally to change ourselves for the better, thus changing the world we perceive. In doing so, we begin to create a new cultural *syntax;* one encouraging us to become *whole.*

PART5: THOUGHTS ON OBTAINING VALUE

BEFORE WE BEGIN

There are no guarantees with the psilocybin experience; it is mutable and can widely vary from the psychospiritual healing type of experience being discussed in this book. Even if we do experience the effects mentioned here, there is still no guarantee they will transform us for the better. This underscores the importance of developing a personal practice with this substance, or at the very least, an understanding of our intentions before using it. It takes a conscious effort and a significant amount of intention to fully obtain the true depth of wisdom and growth available to us through psilocybin mushrooms. But when we make this effort and develop a personal methodology for the use of psilocybin, we can begin to trust in the mushrooms and the healing they offer.

The different methods contained in the following pages are not absolutes. They are guidelines I have worked with in my personal practice to cultivate the type of experience being discussed. You are not concrete and neither is the psilocybin experience. Flow with these ideas as feels right to you and work to develop a unique relationship with the mushroom through personal experience.

RESPECT

Respect is the foundation of any constructive relationship; be it with a practice, person, or medicine. We are entering an exchange with an organism from which we are hoping to garner insight and/or healing. It is important to treat it with respect as we will gain more from the experience in this way. Respect is one of the manners through which we increase our receptivity to the mushroom's lessons about *self* and life as a whole.

> *"It really matters how you regard your guru. If you regard them as a dog, you'll get the transmission of a dog. If you regard them as a normal person then you will get the transmission of a normal person. If you regard them as an enlightened Buddha; as a force of spiritual awakening in your life, in a sense transcending those other elements – which they may also be – but if you hold their inner essence as that enlightening presence then that is the transmission, that is the forward movement you can expect in your life."*
>
> *-Alex Grey at BurningMan 2003[48]*

When we enter an experience—psychedelic or otherwise—with humbleness and respect, we often receive an experience and a lesson concurrently. If we disrespect it and treat it destructively, the experience we receive will likely follow suit. For example, how much good would a marriage offer if one didn't respect their partner?

The source of an experience with psilocybin is not the mushroom itself, it is only the catalyst. The source of the experience is within us. So when we show respect to the experience and the substance that occasioned that experience, we are actually showing respect to an aspect of *self*. This respect for *self* is a key element in utilizing psilocybin for personal growth.

83

MEDITATION

To help increase the potential of having a healing experience, I highly recommend incorporating meditation. The practice of meditation varies widely and offers many different benefits. It is a vast topic; multiple volumes of books have been, and still could be, written on the subject. I won't be attempting to discuss the full breadth of meditation here, but simply touch on its relation to the psychedelic experience.

One lesson a regular meditation practice can bring to our daily life is the release of identification with passing thoughts. This means that while meditating, when thoughts inevitably arise in response to internal or external stimuli, we can choose to observe these thoughts without identifying with them. This allows an observation of our thoughts as simply *being* instead of *being who we are*.

My personal meditation practice is often focused on cultivating an internal state of single-pointed focus on the non-judgmental awareness of my emotional perception. This state of awareness is often cultivated through slow, intentional breathing. It is an incredibly challenging experience with no definite point of success, but learning to be in this quality of awareness on the tides of my emotions has drastically increased my quality of life, as well as the effectiveness of my psychedelic practice. It has enabled me to be more present and stable while participating in the full emotional elements of life unfolding within and without me. This ability is also quite beneficial to psychedelic experiences, particularly those of the mushroom, as a part of encouraging their healing potentials.

When in the mushroom state, many thoughts enter the conscious mind as a result of an emotional process that may not be very comfortable. When we follow those thoughts by relating and identifying with them, it brings us into a perpetual loop of associating personal references to the concepts that surround the emotion at hand. If this emotion is uncomfortable, we begin to limit our ability to move beyond it. If it is a pleasant emotion, following it might be a fun and entertaining intellectual play. In either case, we may be disconnecting from the deeper emotional information communicated through the mushroom-enhanced state. If, like in meditation, we are able to accept all thoughts that come into awareness as simply *being,* and release attachments to them without judgment or entertainment, we are able to stay more centered within the emotional experience. This skill can help us be more present in the emotional honesty of whatever state of consciousness—psychedelic or not—we have chosen to enter, and the potential lessons present within it.

BREATH

When in a direct encounter with elements of ourselves that are deeply challenging, we are immersed in turbulent emotional environments. In order to navigate through this turbulence, it is important to stay as relaxed and open to the experience as possible. This relaxation allows the emotional energy flowing through us to be processed more completely. Along with meditation, breath plays an important role in facilitating this relaxation. It can allow us a fuller *surrender* into the intensity of pending emotional challenges, and thus a fuller processing of undigested emotional energy.

Deep, slow, and intentional breaths, that expand and contract the belly, allow for more oxygen to enter the body, keeping the physiological mechanisms of cellular respiration consistent. When this respiration is consistent, unnecessary tension will not build up in the body or in the mind. When the body and mind are free from allocating energy to unnecessary tension, that energy can be more directly utilized in the process of *emotive-psychosynthesis.*

> *Deep breathing is the tool of the masters for letting go of old attachments and old emotions and for extracting the wisdom hidden within the experiences of life.*
>
> *-Ron Teegaurden*[49]

Do Your Research and Find a Guide

One of the most important aspects to understanding a psychedelic experience with psilocybin mushrooms is earnestly researching the knowledge of others who have investigated this substance, and the psychedelic/mystical experience in general, prior to engaging. This research builds a conceptual foundation allowing us to be more prepared for what we will go through and the information we may receive. Yet, even with a solid base of intellectual research, nothing can fully prepare us for what we will go through or explain exactly how we will experience it. This is why, if it is an option, it can be very beneficial to have a trusted guide during the experience*.

Cultures that use psychoactive substances in *ceremony* have an experienced guide who leads them along their journey. A guide who has not only been trained in the significance of the medicine being used, but one who has used it frequently enough to develop a strong personal relationship with it and an understanding of it. There are a myriad of terms to reference this "guide", but as discussed in Part 2, the popularized term in Western culture is 'shaman'. This term originates from Northern Siberia[50] and was presented as a generalized term to Western academia by Mircea Eliade through his book **Shamanism: Archaic Techniques of Ecstasy**. In Western society, the closest thing we have to the shaman is the psychiatrist, which is quite a stretch in comparison.

The illegality and conditioned paradigm surrounding the use of psilocybin mushrooms in Western culture vastly limits us from developing a strong foundation for their use, or regulated training programs to educate people. We are often left in the dark on this subject, unaware of how to find the guidance we may need. It is this cultural ignorance that is the cause for people psychologically damaging themselves through destructive use of psychedelics—damage that books like this one can help mitigate.

---

* However, be aware that without a standardized training program in place, and the forceful criminalization of those who choose to work with this substance, there is no guarantee that a person who claims experience has true wisdom. Be mindful of the risks.

Thankfully, even though this research is widely criminalized and suppressed, the limitations of cultural ignorance have not stopped people from entering and mapping their time in this space. In order to build an understanding through direct experience, these explorers of the inner-world, the psychonauts, are creating a map; a conceptual framework for others to use for navigating the novelty of the psychedelic mind. The work of these explorers has much to offer new and fresh minds regarding safe and responsible use[*]. Remember, without any regulated training, there is no guarantee these explorers have the right answers for us, so be cautious and skeptical.

If you choose to explore the psilocybin mushroom for its healing properties, my personal advice is that it is best to find someone who has direct knowledge of the psilocybin experience. If this is not possible, other options may be having someone to experiment and explore with, someone to help keep the lessons objectively valid. Or, having a small control group of people, who may not take mushrooms but will not judge you, as a grounded point of reference, may be enough to keep you safe in your exploration.

Eventually, you may not need a guide or a journey partner any longer. As we re-enter an exchange with the mushroom, we begin to become familiar with its environment and our own emotional depths, enabling us to more effectively navigate the experience. The *language* we develop begins to hold firmer conceptual ground and we are able to more confidently interact with the poignancy of the psilocybin experience on our own. Still, it is easy to get lost, no matter how familiar one may be with the space. Having someone to talk openly with about these experiences can be very helpful.

---

[*] A great source for this information is **Erowid.com**.

DEFINE INTENTION / ESTABLISH THE SET

Throughout the development of psychedelic psychotherapy research, there has been a recurring theme in learning how to navigate psychedelic experiences: *set, setting,* and *dose.* These three elements play major factors in the caliber of experience we seed for ourselves.

Intention is what we bring to the experience before the experience happens, the *set.* By taking time before entering the experience to define an intention, we *set* an internal point of reference by which we will engage with the experience. When we do this, it is as if we are pre-programming the energetic signature of the upcoming experience emotionally, psychologically and spiritually*.

Before ingesting a substance, it is best to take some time to define our intentions. Try to put it into a single and straightforward statement or question—i.e., "my intention tonight is to explore my relationship with my family", or, "what is causing me to overreact with anger so frequently?" If the intention is confusing or undefined, it leaves room for misunderstanding. I have also found it very important in my practice to sit and hold the mushrooms prior to ingestion and talk to them. I tell them of my hopes and dreams, my fears, and how much I respect them. I code my intention into them by stating, "tonight my intention of journeying with you is [insert intention here]", or by asking them my question. I always conclude this exchange with them in an expression of gratitude and love. I feel practices like this are an important aspect to a mature and constructive use of psychedelic substances, but not necessarily for everybody. That being said, if you are unable to express at least one reason as to why you are choosing to take a substance, perhaps you should not be taking it.

---

* The benefits of intention setting reach much further than psychedelic experiences and can be applicable throughout life.

RELEASE EXPECTATIONS

It may seem counter-productive, but after having taken the time to confidently state and *set* intention, we should completely release any attachments we may have to how those intentions will be addressed and our expectations of them being addressed at all. Without fully understanding the depths of the subconscious, there is no way for us to be able to predetermine how certain issues will be brought up. If we have prior attachments to or expectations of the issues being addressed, those expectations will likely come with a specific idea of how that should happen. And if we hold too firmly onto those expectations, chances are, the lessons will be missed as they pass by, kind of like missing a train because we were preoccupied with watching the other tracks.

CHOOSE YOUR SETTING

With any psychedelic, it is important to consider how an external environment will affect one's inner state of being. The physical environment—*setting*—we choose will have a significant affect on the experience. If the purpose of taking a substance is spiritual practice and/or self-discovery, a quiet, comfortable place is best. In order to release from the external world and journey within, it is beneficial to be in a place where we can feel safe enough to leave the external world behind. Going out to parties or even off into a bustling city can be interesting and engaging experiences, but in order to connect with the inner *self* in a way that helps us to understand what is happening within, it is important not to be too distracted by what is going on outside of us.

I have come to realize that, for me, the *setting* that best facilitated the type of experience being discussed in this book was an outdoor journey. If that was not a comfortable option due to weather conditions, excess distractions, or safety concerns, the best choice was somewhere indoors. I liked to dedicate a room to the journey and establish that room's specific purpose through personal *ceremony*. Examples of this included cleaning the room first, preparing a notebook and some water, soft music, dimming the lights, and burning some sage or incense. I have, however, experimented with a variety of different *settings* as I felt these different settings would help expose different aspects of myself that could only shine in certain contexts.

When taking mushrooms I preferred not to be around other people who have not taken them as well, unless they were a dedicated sober sitter. Being around others who are not on psychedelics changes the experience. For example, if one is high and in a room of sober people, depending on the *dose*, the *meaningfulness* of one's trip might be referenced by the group's sobriety and could result in a lack of intensity or heightened feeling of discomfort. Regardless of what the specific *setting* we may choose, what is most important for intentional psychospiritual healing is to choose somewhere calm, comfortable, and safe.

DOSE

The question of *dose* is very important and also very particular. The correct *dose* is essentially defined by personal experience and is dependent on what level of depth one wishes to journey. In the experiments at Johns Hopkins University, where psilocybin was found to occasion "experiences similar to spontaneously occurring mystical experiences"[51], Roland Griffiths provided his patients with 30mg of pure psilocybin per 70kg of body weight[52]. Terrance McKenna often referred to five grams of dried mushrooms as a "heroic dose"[53]. Among the people I have met in my life, two dried grams is often standard. For my personal practice, I had found between three and four dried grams to be the most constructive. I wanted to be fully engaged by the experience, but not so incapacitated by novelty that I couldn't bring something applicable back from it.

The manner in which I would prepare the mushroom varied, but I often steeped it in a tea with other herbs such as Guayusa and Reishi. For the most potent experience, I found that taking this tea while hot and blending it with Cacao Powder, He Shou Wu, Honey, and a fat such as

Coconut Oil or Cacao Butter is very effective. I have found this method to increase the potency of the experience while being relatively easier on my stomach.

The LD50 for psilocybin, which is the lethal dosage for 50% of a test group, is 285 mg/kg i.v. (intravenous) for mice, 280 mg/kg i.v. for rats, and 12.5 mg/kg i.v. for rabbits [54]. According to math done by **TheShoomery.org**, "using the data for rats and accepting a median of 1% potency, [...] it would require the consumption of 1680g of mushrooms to reach the *LD50* for a 60kg rat. This amount of mushrooms is enough to provide a 'normal' mushroom trip to roughly 650 people."[55] In other words, there isn't much to worry about in terms of the potential for a physical overdose.

With that being said, it is important to remember that though we may not be able to physically overdose on psilocybin mushrooms, it is possible to consume enough to provide a much stronger experience than we are able to handle psychologically. It is also possible to eat enough to cause significant indigestion—the stomach can't always deal well with large amounts of foreign foods. I would never recommend for anybody to take more than five dried grams. The most I have ever eaten is eight dried grams, and it was amongst the most intense experiences of my life. Be cautious, be safe, and be responsible.

GUT ROT AND PREPARATION SUGGESTIONS

It is very common among psilocybin users to experience indigestion from the mushrooms. Often called "gut rot", it can be quite a negative experience for some, creating unnecessary levels of anxiety and discomfort. There are a few things one can do in order to reduce the symptoms of indigestion. The first is to make the mushrooms into a tea or a decoction*, which makes it much easier on the stomach since it is no longer required to digest the mushroom flesh. The mushrooms are broken

---

* Decoction is a hot water method of extracting medicinal components from herbs.

into small pieces and gently simmered for about twenty minutes. The remaining mushroom pieces are then strained out and the decoction is mixed with other teas according to personal herbal preferences. For an extra reduction of indigestion, preparing this decoction with ginger root is wonderful! The world of tea is a one of sacred herbal alchemy; there is much to explore – have fun.

Another option is to prepare the mushrooms in chocolate. The trick to chocolate preparation is to ensure the dried product is ground down as finely as possible, into a dust. The mushroom dust is mixed in with some type of chocolate that has been melted with a double boiler. Once the dust has been fully mixed in, the chocolate can be laid out onto a tray or into molds. These chocolates can keep a long time if frozen in proper containers. Or, try adding some chocolate powder to tea to make a magic hot chocolate! I have found chocolate helps to soften the physical consequences of eating psilocybin mushrooms, while also increasing the potency of the experience. My preference was to work with certified organic raw chocolate products, but simple grocery store baker's chocolate works great and costs less. However, I think raw chocolate might be a secret to enabling powerful experiences that are relatively easy on the body and mind.

If the choice is to simply eat raw mushrooms, my suggestion to is to chew them really, really well. Chewing is the first stage of mechanical digestion; we will find a big difference in the digestive process if we chew well, in all areas of life. The mushrooms may not taste "good" according the conditioned flavor preference most of us have, though it makes a world of difference when we chew them down to a mush (pun intended) before we swallow it. Besides reducing indigestion, this also helps to release the active alkaloids from the mushroom to be absorbed through the mouth and directly into the blood stream, helping with uptake.

Regardless of what method of ingestion we choose, there may still be varying levels of indigestion. The suggestion I can give here is to change the *meaningfulness* consciously given the sensations arising from the stomach. A common automatic response to indigestion is to try to make it go away. This response is normally appropriate as indigestion is a sign of poor eating choices. When it arises in response to having eaten psilocybin mushrooms, however, it is a marking point for one's intentional entrance into a new state of consciousness. It can be celebrated and honored, or at least accepted and *surrendered* to. This change in the *meaningfulness* attributed to the indigestion will change, for the better, the way it manifests in one's experience.

ONSET

Surrender is a key element to obtaining high levels of personal value from the psilocybin experience, yet in order to fully *surrender*, one needs to feel safe in both their external and internal environments. One of the main hindrances to maintaining a sense of inner-safety is the potentially intense physical sensations that arise during psilocybin's onset. The body begins to enter a fight or flight response and we may feel a rushing sensation inside of us. If we are not familiar with the experience, it is easy to become overwhelmed and allow emotional states to become erratic before the psilocybin has taken full effect. This is why it is important to be calm during the onset of this experience and trust that we are safe, even though the body is in fight or flight.

I often found the metaphor of a plane taking off to be effective in conceptually navigating a heavy onset. As the psilocybin takes effect, imagine it is an airplane starting its ascent—suddenly accelerating, turbulent, and maybe producing feelings of vertigo. This is only the onset and just like an airplane, the physical sensation begins to calm down and, aside from occasional turbulence, will ease once cruising altitude is reached.

Considering Emotional Awareness

The psilocybin experience is founded within one's emotional being. Yet, there is a conceptual disconnect between the rational mind and the emotional being, which can generate a lot of confusion. It is important to remember that specifics of a mushroom experience as *languaged* by the mind are products of attempting to make rational sense of an experience that transcends its familiar reality structure. Numerous ideas come through one's conscious mind during this experience, and many may not make sense outside of the altered state that inspired them. This is because the altered state is one of deep emotional awareness, which is inherently non-rational. Focusing too much on the ideas, hallucinations, or visions arising from the very unfamiliar territory of emotional depth can be confusing to the sober, rational mind, and difficult to integrate into everyday life.

One method of avoiding the entertainment of novel visions received throughout deep personal work is asking, "what is my emotional state right now?", "how do I relate to these emotions?", and/or "what are these emotions showing me about myself?". I have found these questions important for keeping my journey on track and my rational mind grounded even in the midst of completely non-rational experiences. Usually the experience will redirect one's perspective with these questions, helping the experience to be more personally relevant. It's important to note, however, I am not saying the conceptual manifestations of emotional states during a psilocybin experience should be ignored. The lessons we receive are not necessarily in the details of that experience; they are the experience itself. This means the details are not as important as the big picture: which can be demonstrated with the question: "who am I now, in relation to a psychedelic awareness of my deeply unconscious emotional identity?"

Develop a Relationship and a Practice with the Mushroom

It takes time and practice to learn how to interact with the experiential characteristics of psilocybin, and to determine what aspects of *self* will shine through. It is important to build and participate in a personal relationship with those experiential characteristics. Over time the mushroom becomes like a friend, who with respect and love, we enjoy the company of; one who knows more about us than we know about ourselves. A friend that delivers the most personal, intimate, and compassionate exchange of tough love, constructive criticism, playful expression, sensual pleasure, and contemplative wonder. A friendship expressed on the scale of one's vastly expanding imagination.

Since the mushroom is bringing aspects of *self* to a surface awareness, when we develop a relationship of respect and trust with it, we are developing a relationship of respect and trust with our *self*. This will not only deepen the honesty and poignancy of the lessons we experience, but also set a habit to express that same level of respect and trust across many different avenues of life.

RELEASING RELUCTANCE

Before we begin to develop a deep trust in a relationship with the mushroom, we often resist the lessons presented within the experience. The majority of our self-identification is based upon the same conditioning the mushroom experience dissolves. So, it is easy to be hesitant to accept anything it reveals that is counter to our previously established identity.

Sometimes the mushroom guides us into emotional environments we didn't know existed, places we hadn't prepared ourselves for, and shows us aspects of *self* we don't want to deal with. Some of these places might be so feared we don't want to go into them, so we resist the confrontation of a direct experience. It is this resistance that agitates anxiety and confusion. Being overly attached to resisting a potentially inevitable caliber of experience creates the relative observation of suffering, which inspires anxiety and "bad trips"—i.e., "I don't want to directly experience my *shadow*".

This is where the importance of practicing *surrender* comes in to facing these challenges. Without it, we risk learning nothing from the pain of *facing the shadow*. When we release the reluctance to accept *what is* and *surrender*, we allow this process to move more smoothly—not necessarily more comfortably. Remember, it is both the mushroom and a deeper aspect of *self* that have generated the context of the experience, and whatever challenge we may face is necessary for personal growth. Trust it, there is value there.

A Lanuage for Better Communication

Being guided into the depths of our full emotional potency with psilocybin mushrooms, far beyond any experiential understanding we have stored in the conditioned mind, can be very confusing at first. Though as we revisit and explore this state, we develop a personal *language* that enables the conscious mind to interpret the information psilocybin releases from the subconscious. This *language* makes it much easier to learn from these experiences.

Developing a *language* to communicate with the subconscious through the use of mushrooms has an effect on one's personality as a whole. It sets a relative point of self-awareness that echoes out into many other facets of life. As we actively learn this *language*, and how to work with it, the subconscious simultaneously learns how to communicate better with the conscious mind, like a balanced and beautiful feedback loop of energetic symbiosis. It seems as though responsible use of this psychedelic expands one's mind to be more perceptive and effective in communicating with the deeper aspects of *self* in general.

Come Down, Revisit, and Contemplate

When on psilocybin, everything looks and feels vastly different than it does in an ordinary state of mind. We begin to experience the world in a very new and creative way. Because of the potentially confusing information that comes out of a psilocybin experience, there is a tendency for people to see their experience as being too "strange" to be applicable to their daily lives. This results in the experience being trivialized—"it was just a trip"—and thus omitted from life's lessons, even if the experience of this "trip" could potentially provide a great deal of personal growth. The practice of *come down, revisit, and contemplate* helps to address this.

Come down from the trip and back into normal, waking reality. Yes, the experience was profound and important, but it is only a partial segment of life. We have other roles and responsibilities outside of the psychedelic space that we are accountable for—i.e., a job, bills, personal projects, food, shelter, and maintaining healthy relationships. There are elements of waking reality that require us to be present, and people who count on us. Many of these roles and responsibilities may be called into question during a psilocybin experience and we shouldn't ignore that. But to truly benefit from such a mind-altering experience, its lessons needs to be integrated into the holistic context of everyday waking life.

I used to think the psychedelic state was the ultimate reality and that in order to be a fully evolved spiritual being, I needed to be in that state as often as possible. I felt as though there was a truth in this state that needed to be lived. This was naive thinking, an expression of substance abuse, and an unconscious ego technique for evading the emotional responsibility of being accountable in life. Thankfully, I realized that no matter how high I got, and no matter how much of an expression of "ultimate reality" the psychedelic experience may be, unless I learned to become *whole* in the context of my everyday life, I would never develop honest psychospiritual maturity.

The heart beats, and the lungs breathe in the here and now, but the mind often wanders. Wherever it wanders, the emotional being follows and that internal space becomes the point of reference by which we experience reality. *Revisit* is like a conscious process of psychic time-travel; we use the memory to bring the conscious mind back to the space we were in during the time of the trip. To *revisit* the emotional states occasioned by psilocybin, even if they were difficult, establishes a familiarity and strengthens those experiences into long-term memory. When we do this, the lessons inherent in those amplified emotional states become clearer and easier to integrate.

Contemplate psilocybin experiences with the rational mind. Most lessons you learn while on mushrooms can be cryptic and symbolic, but there are still clear messages being shouted directly at us. It is important to consider what decisions these messages may be encouraging, and how those decisions may affect our lives from a sober perspective. Like intuition, these psychedelic experiences can offer an "ah-ha, eureka!" moment that sparks a wonderful new direction in life. However, it is important to consider whether or not that new direction leads us towards the personal goals we have set for ourselves. Sometimes these psychedelic micro-epiphanies can work as the experiential point of reference by which we more confidently make a choice that is counter to those epiphanies. It is important to consider our choices with a clear mind before we make changes or take actions based on the experiences of psilocybin or any psychedelic substance. At the same time, part of these experiences is to cultivate the courage to step outside our comfort zone, so do not be afraid to take calculated risks.

As a personal example, while meditating during psilocybin *ceremony* at the lunar eclipse of the 2010 winter equinox, I came to realize I needed to move out of the home I had only recently moved into with my best friends. Living with them was the result of long-set plans and had been very important to each of us. I had even moved away from a wonderful life in Ontario to achieve this in Alberta. While taking witness to the moon cast in vibrant reds, I became overwhelmingly aware of how living there was holding me back from the personal passions I wanted to realize in my life. However, it was terrible timing: four days before Christmas, three days before my housemate's birthday, ten days before the new year, followed by a two week out-of-town holiday in January. This was a very difficult context to not only inform my best friends I was moving out, but to then go find a new home.

So, I waited a few days, weighed my options, and considered what would be required of me to make this happen. Ultimately, I decided to go for it. I'm very glad I did, because not only did it drastically increase my personal sense of well being, it saved my friendships with those former housemates. In this specific experience, I decided to take a leap of faith based on a psychedelic epiphany, but only after I took some time to *come down, revisit,* and *contemplate* its implications in my life. I hope it shows that it is important to not make rash decisions, but it is also important not to be afraid to take a risk if it feels right in your heart.

EMBODY MENTALITY

Returning from the journey of a psilocybin-enhanced emotional experience and taking time to *revisit* and *contemplate* helps us to effectively plant its lessons in the mind. But in order to truly benefit from this experience, it is important to learn to live in accordance with those lessons. We do this by learning to trust in the honesty of the emotional experience it occasioned, and apply the lessons learned from it by living the embodiment of what we have learned.

Live the mentality developed through exploring *self* with psilocybin, let it inspire the person we choose to be. It is more than simply new ideas, powerful emotions, and novel experiences to think about. Directly apply that which is learned about *self* into everyday life.

SHARING WITH OTHERS

When something profound and beautiful happens to us we will often be inspired to share it with others, especially if it comes with a sense of personal empowerment. Nevertheless, when it comes to experiences had through psilocybin mushrooms, this can be a tricky situation. In most of Western society, we have been conditioned to trivialize and, somewhat paradoxically, demonize psilocybin and psychedelics in general. We are conditioned to make people feel uncomfortable, alienated, and like something is wrong with them if they express any type of drug use that isn't culturally accepted like alcohol, tobacco, coffee, sugar, etc. Because of this conditioning there is a fear that if we openly share our use of unaccepted substances, we will be led to feel like something is wrong with us and we will jeopardize social status in some way. So we say nothing; we suppress the inspiration to share openly with others. Unfortunately, most of the time the choice to say nothing about our substance use is likely the most responsible one we can make to protect ourselves. If we are invested into something like a salary job, we likely want to maintain that investment's integrity.

Just because it may be the most responsible choice not to discuss our use of psilocybin in the public sphere, doesn't mean we can't share the inspirational revelations and wonder we experienced. We don't have to explain to someone the intimate details of a mushroom journey to communicate that which we have learned from it, in fact, doing so may block the shared lesson being received openly. As a sad result of cultural indoctrination, many people immediately disregard any lessons learned from a "drug" experience simply because they have already decided they don't agree with the source; regardless of how applicable it may be to their lives or how much they may otherwise agree with it. But the psilocybin experience is only one facet of life; the lessons that come out of it are broad-reaching and founded on an honest expression of *self*. When interacting in a highly conditioned social situation, there is no need to allow well-earned wisdom to be culturally circumscribed by attributing it to a psychedelic journey. It was not the journey that created the wisdom; it was only the catalyst for discovery.

So let's embody the mentality arising from these psychedelic discoveries and express them through who we are, instead of what we've done. Remember: example teaches better than explanation, and as Neal Goldsmith puts it, "there's a big difference between a spiritual experience and a spiritual life"[56].

All that being said, *nothing would ever change if no one chose to make a confident stand for something they believed in.* The cultural stigma and conditioning surrounding psilocybin and other psychedelics will not change if we do not chose to speak confidently, intelligently, and maturely about their potential.

DON'T TAKE YOURSELF TOO SERIOUSLY

One of the most recurring lessons I have learned is that even though what is being addressed with the mushroom is important and needs to be respected, it doesn't mean we need to get too serious about it. The process of aggressively self-policing based on what I learned through psilocybin is something I went through on a regular basis. Through that, I learned it is important to be consistent, respectful, and diligent in this practice; but it is also important to be easy on ourselves. We may be faced with challenging experiences and address serious topics, but ultimately those challenges help to process inner-hardships and enable us to discover how to experience the lighter side of life with more fullness and creativity. Don't loose sight of the true value by getting wrapped up by the work it involves.

PART 6: OTHER THOUGHTS

BAD TRIP VS. HARD TRIP

"There's no such thing as a bad trip" is a concept that is rising in popularity among experienced drug users. However, I don't subscribe to this concept. To me, there is such a thing as a *bad trip* and it is determined by how we choose to deal with an uncomfortable experience. This choice determines whether the challenges we face during a psychedelic encounter will be a *bad trip* or a *hard trip,* which are two qualitatively different experiences.

A *bad trip* is when we become overwhelmed by an anxiety resulted from the resistance of an altered state—i.e., wishing we were not high anymore, or wishing the experience were different. This is usually a result of taking drugs without an understanding what we are getting ourselves into, inappropriate dosage, or taking drugs in a destructive environment. As a *bad trip* subsides, often there has been no lesson learned and we, relieved to be free of that "bad" experience, are quick to leave it all behind and forget the experience altogether. Not all *bad trips* are that bad, but they certainly aren't very enjoyable. The elements that create a *bad trip* and their consequences can often be avoided by knowledgeable use and proper guidance.

A *hard trip* is when we are presented with the darker aspects of *self*, the *shadow*. But instead of resisting the discomfort of that encounter, we embrace it, we *surrender* to it. It is these *trips* that hold the most potential for personal growth. And learning how to *surrender* into the honesty of emotional experience, especially if it is challenging, enables this growth most effectively. The key difference between these two types of experiences is that during a *bad trip* we close ourselves off to what is being presented; during a *hard trip* we open ourselves up.

For example, the psilocybin mushroom can send us into a full expression of emotional potency. It amplifies whatever emotional state may be present within us at the time, known or unknown, positive or negative. The mind then compiles and brings awareness to all the thought patterns and memories attributed to the *meaningfulness* of the emotional state we are in. If during this process we fixate awareness on feeling uncomfortable by resisting an uncomfortable emotion, we amplify the potency of being uncomfortable in an effort to explain that discomfort to ourselves through various thought patterns, memories, or feelings. If, when confronted with the same uncomfortable emotion, we choose to *surrender* to its presence, we will generate a different *meaningfulness* towards that discomfort. A *meaningfulness* of being healed, for example, will generate a different set of thought patterns and memories. Essentially, whether we go through a detrimental *bad trip* or a beneficial *hard trip* is decided by choices we make—I personally find this very empowering.

Nutritional Benefit

With the slow release of the stronghold cultural stigmas have placed on psychedelic research, we have begun to re-initiate important investigations into psychedelics. One such example is that of Dr. Robin Carhart-Harris at Imperial College, London. At the time of writing, he is heading a team using functional magnetic resonance imaging (fMRI) to observe the brain on psilocybin in real-time. Through investigating how psilocybin affects the brain in regards to blood flow and general functioning, his research is giving us some very important insight on the neurology of the psilocybin experience. This is just one example of the investigations happening at this time and though the reach of psychedelic research is expanding beautifully, there is still much to investigate.

An area I am very interested in, but where we still lack sufficient understanding, is that of brain nutrition regarding psilocybin—i.e., what nutrients are being utilized, in which ways, and to what results. The ideas of two people from very different areas of study, Cameron Adams and Daniel Vitalis, have presented hypotheses with interesting correlations. From personal experience and a significant understanding of nutrition, I feel these hypotheses deserve consideration.

In his lecture **How Do Psychedelics Heal,** given to the Student Psychedelic Society at the University of Kent in 2010, Cameron Adams addressed the role psychedelics play in the human physiological system, brain health, and physiological evolution. Referencing monoamine tryptamines such as psilocybin and psilocin, he discusses how the brain functionally communicates information via neurotransmitters. These neurotransmitters require substantial nutrition through a variety of foods in order for the body to produce them. Lacking proper nutrition thus results in a lack of neurotransmitters, which he correlates to decreased brain function.

Adams mentions how mental and emotional stress produces a biochemical response within the body that includes the production of the hormone cortisol. Over time, excessive cortisol production results in the slow degradation of the body, first by depleting the brain's neurotransmitter reserves. He proposes that neurotransmitters act as a "buffer" to protect the body from the destructive effects of cortisol. But when we lack the proper nutrition to replenish the brain's neurotransmitter reserves, the result will be decreased cognition, decreased mood, and eventually, the breakdown of different physiological functions.

According to Adams, psilocin acts as a monoamine neurotransmitter and while it is being used, the brain doesn't need to use its own neurotransmitter reserves. After the brain metabolizes psilocin and breaks it down into smaller components, he claims we are left with the nutrients required for building more neurotransmitters[57]. Therefore, not only does the brain apparently get to take a break from using energy to produce its own neurotransmitters, but it is also nourished in its production of more[*]. This increases the brain's neurotransmitter reserves and increases its stress buffer. According to Adams, "taking psychedelics may produce a buffer zone to help us deal with stress and [...] stress-based illnesses or diseases."[58]

Adams also discusses the potential evolutionary benefits this increase of exogenous neurotransmitters in the diet may have for the human species:

> If the energetic or nutritional intake exceeds what you need, you do a little bit better [...] Walking bipedally [sic] seems to have saved our ancestors one little package of Mcvities digestive biscuits worth of calories in a year and that was enough to make [walking upright] more valuable to our ancestors, made them more likely to reproduce, get food [and] be healthier than their four legged friends. [...] Taking exogenous neurotransmitters would be the same sort of caloric and nutritional change and difference.[59]

Daniel Vitalis also speaks of the nutritional benefits of psychedelic mushrooms. Vitalis is a specialist in wild food and nutrition, a nature-based philosopher, and holds public lectures on the significance of diet and habitat as it relates to psychological and physical health. In a lecture I attended, **SurThrival in the 21st Century**, he spoke of how we can recreate a more "natural habitat"[†] for ourselves in the entirely unnatural

---

[*] An interesting correlation to my theory on *emotive-psychosynthesis*. Could this a nutritional correlation to why one often feels so fresh after a psilocybin mushroom experience?

[†] He specifically discusses how habitat is more than just physical surroundings; it includes mental-emotional environment, community members, and available foods.

setting of urban life. This lecture focused deeply on eating foods that were in line with our genetic heritage to ensure the body is nourished by the foods it evolved to require. He spoke strongly for eating foods that are closer to their wild genetic strain, rather than domesticated strains—such as heirloom vegetables and wild game meat over plump supermarket vegetables and factory-farmed meats. He proposes that the lack of nutrition in conventional food, relative to that of wild food, plays a significant role in the modern person's lack of physical and psychological vitality, and the abundance of degenerative diseases currently present in the human species. He feels that changing habitat and diet to be more in line with our unique genetic heritage will help to revitalize us as a species.

In speaking of cultivating vitality though eating in accordance to genetic heritage, he spoke of psychedelic mushrooms. He discussed similar nutritional reasons as Adams for eating these mushrooms, but he also brought up another point that resonated strongly with me. Human culture has been ingesting psychedelically psychoactive plants as a part of their diet for thousands of years. It is only in the last several hundred years that we have removed ourselves from this tradition[*]. Essentially, Vitalis claimed that if we are not ingesting some kind of psychedelically psychoactive plant, then we have a nutritional deficiency in our diet[60]. He also speaks of more than just eating these plants, but also to keep in accordance with the cultural traditions of *ceremony* and to treat these medicines with a value of respect—a perspective I strongly agree with.

If eating psilocybin mushrooms is eating in accordance to our genetic heritage as human beings, as well as an evolutionary advantage to brain health and cognition, we could start to conceptualize a broader perspective on why psilocybin contains such potential for personal healing and growth. Not only does it help us to address repressed emotions while opening us up to the magical wonder of life experientially, it also nourishes the brain's ability to physically maintain the beneficial results of those experiences.

---

[*] A result I believe to be inspired by the initial conditioning set forth by Christian puritanical values that are still deeply seated in Western culture today.

SITTING IN SILENCE

Chances are, if we live in a city, we live in chaos. This is not intended to imply that our lives are chaotic, but that the unfolding world around us is full of the energy of *city living*: fast-paced, condensed, and rapidly changing. Being in this type of environment causes us to think in a similar manner. Our thoughts run a mile a minute and usually without much intentional direction. This distracts us from what might be happening within *self* at levels deeper than that of the compulsively thinking mind. After an extended time of being of in the midst of such a chaotic environment, we almost completely loose connection to this deeper *self* because these ongoing chaos-inspired thought patterns clouding that connection. It is as if the constant influx of chaotic information creates a mental backlog that must be sorted through before we can connect with what's beneath it.

David Deida, a philosopher who speaks on spiritual maturity, says that in order to give our 'deepest gift to the world', which to him is one of the purposes of being alive, we must connect with our 'deepest truth'. To be able to connect with that 'truth', we must put ourselves in silence until the sounds that the world has left ringing through the mind quiet long enough for us to hear our 'deepest essence' speaking to us. He says that for some, this is found in a daily meditation practice, while for others it could be periodic month-long stays at a monastery.[61]

If the point of this silence is to connect with what is happening deep within oneself, I have found the same benefit in a psilocybin practice. When this practice is with mature intention and a respect towards the medicine being used, and we take time out of our lives to sit in *ceremony* with it, we help to amplify the message the deeper *self* is attempting to communicate. Psilocybin helps us to circumvent chaos-inspired thought patterns and process through the cognitive sludge preventing the message of the deeper *self* from being understood. I believe it allows us to connect with this 'deepest truth' Deida speaks of—a connection with who we are, who we want to be, and what we have to 'gift' to the world.

GETTING THERE WITHOUT DRUGS

I have spoken at length about the benefits of psilocybin mushrooms for psychospiritual growth; they allow us to dissolve psychological conditioning, work through repressed emotions, and connect with deeper aspects of *self*. All the while they guide us into the next stage of psychospiritual maturity. Unfortunately, common cultural values of stigma and demonization cause many people to maintain a short-sighted view of these potentials. In expressing my perspective on this issue openly, I have met a lot of opposition from a variety of people. Often this opposition is founded on ideas about psychoactive substances that are not based on personal experience, but cultural stigma, assumption, and a fear of drugs in general. In regards to using psilocybin for spiritual growth, one of the most common counter-perspectives I have heard is that using drugs to help realize a greater spiritual awareness is somehow "cheating". I can understand why people would have that perspective, since we are indoctrinated to resist things we don't understand. However, this type of perspective is fundamentally inaccurate and incomplete.

I certainly support the idea that one does not absolutely need psilocybin to obtain a spiritual experience or a spiritual-awareness of life. I do, however, believe it can help when used responsibly and with spiritual intentions. Psilocybin chemically alters one's perception of reality into a spiritual state of consciousness, allowing that state to be more available to the conscious mind, once one is familiar with it. Psilocybin generates an experience that helps create the neurological pathways necessary for enabling spiritual thought. It also helps provide a conceptual platform for investigating and integrating the implications of spiritual thought into life through a direct and highly personal experience.

I often offer the concept that it is difficult to go to some place if we don't know where that place is. But once someone takes us there and we know what it looks like, it is much easier to find our way back. If we apply this concept to psilocybin and spiritual growth, it doesn't seem like cheating at all. Making our way back to this place, spiritual awareness, still requires a lot of personal work, discipline, and dedication to develop a full understanding of our spiritual nature, regardless of how many times we get a sneak peak at what it looks like.

Judging, trivializing, or denouncing another person's spiritual practice based on ignorance, *fear*, and predetermined values of what is and isn't 'spiritual', is about as far away from living a spiritual life as it gets. Yes, one can get there without drugs, and yes, one can incorporate drugs into getting there. But one cannot get there by *judging* others and considering oneself "more spiritual".

DAGOBAH AS A PROVERB FOR THE PSYCHEDELIC JOURNEY

Within the depths of *self* we find the *Shadow*: the personification of what we wish to avoid facing about ourselves[62], the portion of ourselves we fear most, the source of fear itself. When we block *emotive-psychosynthesis* of the *shadow* by avoiding personal accountability for its presence within us, we generate emotional repression. These repressed aspects of the *shadow* are then projected across the perception of reality as we unconsciously offload the responsibility of fault for the *shadow*. We repress and project because we are afraid of the *shadow; the dark side* of *self*. This *fear* influences us to avoid bearing witness to these *shadow* projections, and instead, we generate a false perception of danger towards anything that may rouse a direct awareness of *shadow*. The body physiologically reacts to this false perception of danger and generates a stress response. The mind also reacts to this false perception and the ego engages in preprogrammed evasion mechanisms, causing us to retreat within, or to lash out. Self-doubt, passive-aggressiveness, *judgment*, arrogance, self-deprecation, and general anxiety are all expressions of the *chronic fear* resulting from avoiding responsibility for the *shadow*. Psilocybin mushrooms can guide us into the *shadow,* help us to face it directly, and facilitate the *emotive-psychosynthesis* needed to grow through *chronic fear*. From this experience, we discover the courage and strength to navigate the *shadow* in daily life.

I can see a parable for *facing the shadow* with psilocybin in the story of Luke Skywalker training with Yoda in the Dagobah swamps in *Star Wars Episode V: The Empire Strikes Back*. In it, Luke Skywalker—a young Jedi warrior in training—goes to a swamp planet in a star system called Dagobah. Luke is seeking a Jedi master named Yoda so that he can also learn to become a Jedi, an enlightened warrior of *The Force*. In Star Wars, *The Force* is the ethereal energy that flows through all things throughout the universe. It is the energetic source of all life, and through practice, can be channelled to accomplish great feats and develop significant supernatural powers. The concept of *The Force* parallels a variety of different philosophies on universal energy like *Prana, Chi, Qi, Reiki, The Quantum Field, God, Love*, etc. There is two ways one can embody *The Force*: with the *light side*, or with the *dark side*. To embody the *dark side* is to use the power of *The Force* for self-serving purposes. The path of the *dark side* eventually leads a Jedi into becoming obsessed with this power. The *dark side* inspires corruption and destruction. It is a representation of what constitutes the cultural values of evil. A Jedi gives into the *dark side* when they loose their *self* to the darkness within. A Jedi becomes consumed by their darkness because they has not learned the truth of its presence by facing it with courage.

At the depth of Luke's training in the Dagobah swamps, Yoda brings him to a cave and tells him that it is strong with the *dark side* of *The Force*. Luke is encouraged to release his weapons and go inside.

Yoda: That place is strong with the dark side of the force, a domain of evil it is, and you must go.
Luke: What's in there?
Yoda: Only what you take with you.[63]

Due to a lack of self-confidence and trust in *The Force* that is flowing through him, Luke ignores the guidance of Yoda and enters with his weapons. Deep within the cave, he finds himself face-to-face with Darth

Vader, a great Jedi who gave into the *dark side,* Luke's greatest nemesis. In a battle between them, Luke cuts off Darth Vader's head only to realize that the face behind Vader's mask is his own.

So how is this story a parable of *facing of the shadow* using psilocybin mushrooms?[*] From a psychedelic perspective, we can see the Dagobah swamps as a representation of the psyche, and the different places Luke trains within the swamps as different emotional environments within the subconscious. Yoda is the ambivalent voice of guidance, the voice of the psilocybin-enhanced intellect; he is the *teaching voice* of the mushroom. There is even a physical correlation to the mushroom, as Yoda is a small creature with a large head that lives in a swamp.

Yoda exposes Luke to new ways of understanding himself by confronting him with different mental-emotional challenges throughout different areas of the swamp. During his training, Yoda helps Luke better integrate these new experiences into his journey of becoming a Jedi. Like the creative ideas and metaphors generated within a psilocybin journey, Yoda speaks to Luke in parables. He does not tell Luke what to think or explain what his experiences mean. He only guides Luke through the swamp while providing perspective on how to consider the challenges within these new environments and how they relate to *The Force* and to developing a connection with it. While sitting on Luke's back, Yoda guides him through the swamp like the psilocybin-enhanced inner-monologue guides us through the emotional environment of the subconscious. Yoda speaks with an enlightened knowledge of *The Force,* constantly presenting Luke with new ideas to consider. Like psilocybin, Yoda's guidance inspires Luke with alternative ways of seeing the significance of his internal experience in relation to the energy of the universe, but does not directly explain to Luke what it all means.

Like many of us, Luke is a resistant student who often holds tight to maintaining control out of a lack of trust in himself and his connection

---

[*] Dear Star Wars fans, please do not take offense. I do not mean to imply that this perspective on the story is the intention of George Lucas or the deeper meaning of the story itself.

with *The Force*. He resists *surrender* to his wise teacher. This lack of trust and *surrender* makes it difficult for Luke to grasp the simplicity of Yoda's teachings and is often the source of Luke's confusion and frustration— similar to what some may consider a "bad trip". Over time, Luke learns to release his resistance to the simplicity of these teachings the same way we learn to *surrender* to the honesty of an emotional experience with psilocybin.

When Yoda—a personification of the wise inner-voice unlocked with psilocybin—brings Luke to the cave, he has brought Luke to face the *shadow*. The cave is the source of Luke's fear, self-doubt, and everything he wishes to avoid about himself. Asking Luke to release his weapons is a metaphor for *surrendering* the ego's constructed defence mechanisms and learning the ability to face his *shadow* from a personal power sourced in *The Force*—the *All That Is, All At Once*. The ego's defence mechanisms are the psychological functions that prevent the conscious mind from directly facing great emotional challenges. When we repress the emotional aspects of *self* we do not want to deal with, the ego works like an automatic security guard to keep these aspects repressed, preventing us from having to deal with the painful truth of our repression.

When Luke enters the cave still holding his weapons, it is another expression of his reluctance to release control and *surrender* to Yoda's wisdom. It is the presence of his ego defences—his weapons—that creates his anxious and inevitably failed confrontation with Vader, who is a unique personification of his *shadow*. Luke fights this personification with his weapons instead of a strength channelled from *The Force*. He attempts to destroy his *shadow* with the ego instead of learning to accept and integrate it from his spiritual center. When Luke is exposed to the head of Vader and sees it to have his own face, he is being shown that fighting his *shadow* with his ego is fighting himself and this will only result in self-defeat.

Like Yoda helping Luke through the swamp, psilocybin mushrooms help by guiding us through the unfamiliar environment of the subconscious. They encourage us to let down our defences and discover a personal power sourced from deep within. The mushrooms expose us to our power to address the honesty of emotional experiences and help us learn how to face dark challenges within *self* with a confidence and courageousness sourced in the ground of being; the *All That Is, All At Once.*

PSYCHOSOCIAL EVOLUTION

We seem to be embodying mentalities, as individuals and a global community, that allow for the ongoing destruction of planet Earth's ecological integrity. These same mentalities are hindering the ability for us to build real, honest relationships with each other. This is not a coincidence. The manner in which Western civilization is currently structured tears up natural resources—from water and lumber, to human labor— in order to generate profit by using socially conditioned materialism and usury debt. This profit benefits few while costing the masses, both now and the generations to come.

The mentality of this civilization has become a leading cultural *syntax* and is spreading throughout the world, casting its detrimental effects across life on multiple levels—from higher level governmental decisions to personal relationships. Almost every social institution that once existed to help us succeed towards a higher quality of life is transforming into a system of control, perpetuated by the conditioning of false materialism, false scarcity, and false debt. It seems clear to anyone who is able to see beyond this conditioned *syntax* that the direction civilization is headed does not bode well for anyone, and our grandchildren will inherit the consequences of our shitty choices.

The issue of this *syntax* is huge and hardly one that can be covered in a few pages. We are perpetrating a mass cultural mental illness whose symptoms span across many elements of life. We can see the destruction it is causing here and now. We see obscene consumption of useless products generating huge amount of waste. We watch as massive political corruption for profit quickly degrades human rights and freedoms with people too lethargic to stand up and prevent it. This ill *syntax* manifests in our bodies as degenerative diseases. We see the symptoms everywhere: an ongoing cultural addiction to the false realities of television, the mass over-prescription of pharmaceutical drugs, absent parents, homelessness, gentrification, increasingly frequent oil spills with ongoing coverage among media to support oil procurement, decreasing biodiversity and ecological integrity, and the list goes on.

The *language* of materialism, scarcity, and competition, deeply ingrained into the rapidly-growing Western population, is pillaging the rest of the planet in order to sustain itself. Consciously or not, when we as human beings choose to participate in this process by not choosing to transform it, we are perpetuating the destruction of our home and the interpersonal relationships that make life worth living. This choice to participate is influenced by indoctrinated values and conditioned thinking; the same values and conditioning the psilocybin experience helps dissolve. If we, as individuals and as a collective, do not make fundamental changes in the way we are choosing to operate ourselves in life, we are going to be in big trouble. This is a great challenge because it means changing the way we think. But we have the tools to help us do this, and psilocybin is one of them.

Psilocybin takes us to a place within ourselves where we experience an emotional connection to *spirit*, to the *All That Is, All At Once*. This experience often feels as though we have tapped into some kind of divine truth of life. We may not be able to understand exactly what that divine truth of life may be, but the experience of connecting with it changes us from the inside out. It offers a clearer vision of the responsibility we have as being stewards for life on this planet, and the fragile beauty of life in general. When we harness these mushrooms and the lessons they teach us, the experience we are offered dissolves the cultural *syntax* that controls us and opens our eyes to see the lies within ourselves and in the world. The experience offers us the ears to hear a seemingly ambivalent truth that echoes from the heart.

Every choice we make affects everything—seen and unseen. The clearer vision psilocybin can offer is important in choosing a new path for oneself and for the progress of the planet. This path has opened me towards a better understanding of others and their hardships, a result of having addressed the reality of my own hardships. I have seen, in myself and in others, how easy it is to fall back into the cultural *languages* that alienate us from each other, *languages* like selfishness, social competition, aloofness, aggression, dishonesty, *judgment*, and manipulation.

Things are falling apart all over the world and the conditioning of the Western mind is leading the mental illness responsible for this. The hard truth here is that those of us living in the Western world are perpetuating global problems through participation. Not just in buying useless products or watching television, but also by continuing to support, influencing others into, and identifying with unchecked expressions of the culturally conditioned patterns that hurt our relationships to each other and to the world at large. We do have a choice and the power to change things, but first we must realize the truth of the lies we are being told to tell ourselves. It is a realization that can come in many forms, but I have found to be openly granted by the psilocybin mushroom when used in the right context. Mushrooms have enabled changes in me for the better, and I feel they can do the same for others as well.

Every choice we make affects everything—seen and unseen. We do not have to go out and "change the world" to change the world. We only need to change *our* world, to change ourselves, and through honest presence, be a shining example of psychospiritual maturity that inspires others to do the same on their own accord. Maybe this means writing books, maybe it means volunteering with a food bank, maybe it means marching in the streets. What really matters is that we discover the honest expression of our hearts and have the courage to stand up for it. The following short piece, written some time ago, explores this concept:

In regards to a crumbling civilization,

Yes, the established order of deceit and selfish materialistic gain through capitalism operating at the higher levels of organization in our civilization face inevitable collapse under the weight of its own destructive force, but simply accepting and recognizing it will do nothing to help.

The world that we live in is the total sum average of the choices we make and the people we choose to be. Where the world is now is the destructive result of unconscious reactivity to the flooding of self-wealth and abundance that came from industrialization and agriculture. The fact that we can recognize this tension with conscious criticism is a sign of good progress, as it is only when we can recognize tension that we can begin to understand our ability to dissolve it.

I don't mean to imply that we have to begin to learn how to dissolve the tension existing on a worldwide scale. Remember, the world is the sum total average of our choices. So if in our personal lives, with ourselves and with others we are close with — our family, our community — we choose to recognize and move beyond tension into the space surrounding; we are helping to make progress.

Rupert Sheldrake, a cell biologist, suggests that species communicate with each other on the genetic and subconscious level via "morphogenetic fields" and "orphic resonance". What he proposes is that there is a field by which species intercommunicate their development. When one bird of a species learns a new skill that can benefit the survival of the species, by morphic resonance and through these fields, that skill is communicated to all the other birds of that species. Enabling that skill to be more easily learned by all the other birds of that species. So when we learn to dissolve tension in our lives, how to live more compassionately, deal with anxiety or generally progress with intention in our lives we make that a more available option for our entire species, echoing strongest first in those you are closest with.

We are bubbles on the surface, though we are also the water beneath us. Every barrier you dissolve in your life, you help dissolve in the collected mind. Every time you transcend tension and build a new space of compassionate progression, you make that space more available to everyone else.

The progress of quantum physics is beginning to show us in more complete detail that it is observation that creates the perpetuating reality around us. Morphic Resonance shows us how we may be unconsciously communicating that reality between each other to build a common ground. So as we approach a worldwide tension resulting from many poor choices of behavior from our society's forefathers and elders, we need to be aware of what we are bringing out to our fellow (hu)man. Do we want to create only the observation of what's wrong and sit in it like a cold damp wallow, uncomfortable but familiar? If we are to progress into maturity as individuals and as a collective, we have to actively choose and create action, other wise we will not help to pull ourselves beyond neutral.[64]

This piece was an effort to expose people to the power we hold in creating true, lasting change. A power whose depth we learn when we begin to dissolve cultural conditioning and rebuild *self* through the inspiration of personal dreams and visions. If we do not choose to harness this power and use it consciously towards healing *self* and thus the world around us, it will be used against us to further perpetuate destruction. This choice is in our hands; we are responsible for what comes.

PART 7: IN CLOSING

Throughout the course of this book, I have attempted to *language* the conceptual framework for how psilocybin mushrooms helped me change and grow. These mushrooms have helped me break free of many conditioned patterns of self-defeat and deprecation by allowing me to process the emotional repression that had compounded over the course of my life. They enabled me to connect with an aspect of myself that was explained in the religion of my childhood as "God", but that I had never actually experienced. This connection has unlocked a direct awareness of my passions, creativity, and a sense of self-love that fuels my life. But it wasn't the mushrooms that healed me. It was the conscious efforts in setting the stage for my psychedelic journeys, as described in this book, that enabled the mushroom to support my self-healing.

Even with the experience of psychedelics helping me along my journey of self-healing and psychospiritual maturity, I don't believe they are 'The Way', but merely a reference point. Psychedelics can be like getting a temporary glimpse at a map of *self*, offering a fuller perspective on where we've come from and the direction we may be headed. This makes them a powerful ally in a spiritual practice, but not the "end all, be all" of personal development. Everyone has a different path to walk and each of us may discover it in our own way. We may be cut from the same cloth, but we each discover a personal connection to *spirit* and cultivate psychospiritual maturity in our own ways. Through helping cleanse a lot self-doubt and a clouded self-image, psilocybin mushrooms and the experiences that came from my practice with them played a major role in waking up to my inner-power. They offered me the opportunity to discover the courage to accept emotional honesty and a responsibility for my darkness by holding me emotionally accountable for my choices.

I continue to feel confused and lost in life at certain times, and find myself doing things that don't serve or represent me in the way I know, on some level, that I want to be served and represented. But incorporating psilocybin into my spiritual practice—a practice that even without the mushroom has helped me connect with myself—has greatly helped me in becoming more aware of, and better understanding, how my choices serve and represent me. It has helped me to better understand what inspires my choices and the emotional consequences those choices may have. In doing so, psilocybin has granted me an insight into the depth of my decisions making process and enabled me in making choices that are consciously in-line with the person I am discovering I want to be.

Thirteen months after I began my full moon psilocybin practice, I stopped to take an objective look at my life and how I had changed. I saw a sense of maturity and self-esteem I had never seen in myself before. I had come to a point where I was more aware of a personal responsibility for the emotional consequences of my choices and a sense of confidence I hadn't known before. I found that something within was telling me to embody my new sense of self-love into creative passions and gift those passions to the world. I have done my best to live my life in this way, and one of those gifts is this book. I hope you have received it well.

The implications of the psilocybin experience are a vast and complex topic, and I would be fooling myself to think I have it all figured out. I have tried my best to explain what I have learned so far in an effort to create a *language* that communicates the broad-reaching implications this medicine may have for human life; a *language* that can be used to explain this experience it in a manner that enables relatable communication and cultivates understanding. For those who have never taken the mushroom and don't plan to, I hope this book has offered you insight into the experience. For those who have experienced it and are curious to its potential, but have not yet gone as deeply as I have, I hope this offers you a way to journey safely. For those who have journeyed these emotional depths but have returned feeling alienated, this book is an effort to let you know *you are not alone; there are others.*

I hope you have found a sense of intrigue or inspiration in these words. They were inspired by a series of experiences led by a *teacher* who taught me about myself through the once foreign *language* of emotional potency. One of the most important lessons I have learned in life, and the one I'd like to leave you with, is this: Each of us is the center of our own infinite cosmos, and the responsibility of our journey lies upon us. Be wise, be humble, be honest, and most of all, be creative.

Thank you.

NOTES

[1] TheCanadianDaily.ca, *Toronto destroys free community garden*

[2] *GoodReads.com,* s.v. "Siddhārtha Gautama Quotes (Author of Buddha)"

[3] Erowid.com, Erowid *Psilocybin Mushroom Vault: Basics*

[4] Griffiths et al., "Psilocybin can occasion mystical-type experiences having substantial and sustained personal meaning and spiritual significance"

[5] Shroomery.org, *Shroomery – Psilocybin Awareness*

[6] Erowid.com, *Erowid Psilocybin Mushroom Vault: Effects*

[7] McKenna, *Food of the Gods*

[8] Munn, "The Mushroom of Language"; Schulte's and Hofmann, *Plants of The Gods*

[9] Munn, "The Mushroom of Language"

[10] Schultes and Hofmann, *Plants of The Gods*

[11] McKenna, *Food of the gods*

[12] Wasson, "Seeking the magic mushroom: a new york banker goes to Mexico's mountains to participate in the age-old rituals of Indians who chew strange growths that produce visions"

[13] Pinchbeck, *Breaking open the head*

[14] Doblin, "Dr. Leary's Concord Prison Experiment: A 34 Year Follow-Up Study"

[15] Cornell University Law School, *21 USC § 812 - Schedules of controlled substances | Title 21 - Food and Drugs | U.S. Code | LII | Legal Information Institute*

[16] Ibid.

[17] Multidisciplinary Association For Psychedelic Studies, *MDMA-Assisted Psychotherapy*

[18] Alper et al., "Treatment of Acute Opioid Withdrawal with Ibogaine"

[19] Weil, *Cannabis Rx: Cutting Through the Misinformation*

[20] McKenna, *True Hallucinations*

[21] McKenna, *Food of the Gods*

[22] Doblin, "Phanke's 'good Friday experiment' a long term follow-up and methodological critique"

[23] Whitby, *LSD: The Beyond Within*

[24] Doblin, "Phanke's 'good Friday experiment' a long term follow-up and methodological critique"

[25] Griffiths, *Psilocybin as a Therapeutic Agent*

[26] Behavioural Pharmacology Research Unit, *Dr. Roland R. Griffiths*

[27] Griffiths, *Episode 69 – Dr. Roland Griffiths :: Psilocybin and Meditation*

[28] Griffiths et al., "Psilocybin can occasion mystical-type experiences having substantial and sustained personal meaning and spiritual significance"

[29] Ibid.

[30] Griffiths et at., "Mystical-type experiences occasioned by psilocybin mediate the attribution of personal meaning and spiritual significance 14 months later"

[31] Griffiths, *Psilocybin as a Therapeutic Agent*

[32] Griffiths et al., "Mystical Experiences Occasioned by the Hallucinogen Psilocybin Lead to Increases in the Personality Domain of Openness"

[33] Psychometric-success.com, *The 'Big 5' Aspects of Personality;* Griffiths et al., "Mystical Experiences Occasioned by the Hallucinogen Psilocybin Lead to Increases in the Personality Domain of Openness"

[34] Griffiths, *Psilocybin as a Therapeutic Agent*

[35] Slater, "How Psychedelic Drugs Can Help Patients Face Death"

[36] Ram Dass, *Be Here Now*

[37] "Ram Dass, *Ram Dass - Love.Serve.Remember*

[38] Schultes and Hoffmann, *Plants of The Gods*

[39] Stresemann, *DMT: The Spirit Molecule*

[40] Lipton, *The Biology of Belief*

[41] Institute of HeartMath, "HeartMath Systems FAQs…"

[42] Redfield, Murphy and Timbers, *God and the Evolving Universe*

[43] Lipton, *The Biology of Belief*

[44] Trungpa, *Shambhala: The Sacred Path Of The Warrior*

[45] Jung, "Conscious, unconscious, and individuation"

[46] Jung, "Psychology and religion: west and east"

[47] Bible Gateway, *Matthew 7:1-5 NIV – Judging Others*

[48] Grey, *007-Grey: "Art, Love, Family and Psychedelics" (part 1)*

[49] Teeguarden, *The Ancient Wisdom of the Chinese Tonic herbs*

[50] Schultes and Hofmann, *Plants of The Gods*

[51] Griffiths et al., "Psilocybin can occasion mystical-type experiences having substantial and sustained personal meaning and spiritual significance"

[52] Ibid.

[53] Davis, *Terence McKenna's Last Trip*

[54] O'Neil, *The Merck Index: An Encyclopedia of Chemicals, Drugs, and Biologicals,* 14ed

[55] Shroomery, *How Many Dried Mushrooms Would I Have To Eat To Die From An Overdose Of Psilocybin?*

[56] Goldsmith, *Psychedelic Healing: The Promise of Entheogens for Psychotherapy and Spiritual Development*

[57] Adams, *252-"How Do Psychedelics Heal?"*

[58] Ibid.

[59] Adams, *252-"How Do Psychedelics Heal?"*

[60] Vitalis, *Surthrival in the 21st Century*

[61] Deida, *Way of The Superior Man*

[62] Jung, "Conscious, unconscious, and individuation"

[63] Lucas, *Star Wars: Episode V: The Empire Strikes Back*

[64] Jesso, *In Regards to a Crumbling Civilization*

Bibliography

Adams, C. "252 Adams-'How Do Psychedelics Heal?'." *Psychedelic Salon,* Podcast Audio Program. 2010. Web, http://matrixmasters.net/archive/Various/252-AdamsKent2010.mp3.

Alper, K.R., H.S. Lotsof, G.M.N. Frenken, D.J. Luciano, and J. Bastiaans. "Treatment of Acute Opioid Withdrawal with Ibogaine." *The American Journal on Addictions.* no. 8 (1999): 234-42.

Behavioural Pharmacology Research Unit, D. "Dr. Roland Griffiths". Last modified May, 2011. http://www.bpru.org/bio/griffiths.html (accessed January 14, 2012).

Bible Gateway, *s.v.* "Matthew 7:1-5 NIV - Judging Others - "Do not judge, or - Bible Gateway" http://www.biblegateway.com/passage/?search=Matthew+7%3A 1-5&version=NIV (Accessed April 24, 2013)

Cornell University Law School, " 21 USC § 812 - Schedules of controlled substances | Title 21 - Food and Drugs | U.S. Code | LII / Legal Information Institute." Last modified May 2013. http://www.law.cornell.edu/uscode/text/21/812 (Accessed May 21, 2013)

Davis, E. "Terence McKenna's Last Trip." *Wired,* May 2000. http://www.wired.com/wired/archive/8.05/mckenna_pr.html (accessed January 14, 2012).

Deida, D. *The Way of the Superior Man: A Spiritual Guide to Mastering the Challenges of Women, Work, and Sexual Desire.* Boulder, Co.: Sound True Inc., 2006

Dictionary.com, s.v. "Syntax,"
  http://dictionary.reference.com/browse/syntax (Accessed December 8,
  2011)

Doblin, R. E. "Phanke's 'good Friday experiment' a long term follow-up
  and methodological critique." *Journal of Transpersonal Psychology* 23,
  no. 1 (1991): 1-28

-------. ""Dr. Leary's Concord Prison Experiment: A 34 Year Follow-Up
  Study." *Journal of Psychoactive Drugs* 30, no.4 (1998): 419-26

Erowid. "Erowid Psilocybin Mushroom Vault: Basics." Last Modified
  November, 2009.
  http://www.erowid.org/plants/mushrooms/mushrooms_basics.shtml
  (Accessed September 21, 2011)

-----. "Erowid Psilocybin Mushroom Vault: Timeline." Last Modified
  April, 2010.
  http://www.erowid.org/plants/mushrooms/mushrooms_timeline.php
  (Accessed November 13, 2011)

Goldsmith, N. *Psychedelic Healing: The Promise of Entheogens for
  Psychotherapy and Spiritual Development.* Rochester Vt.: Healing
  Arts Press, 2011

Goodreads.com, s.v. "Siddhārtha Guatama Quotes (Author of Buddha)"
  http://www.goodreads.com/author/quotes/2167493.Siddh_rtha_
  Gautama (Accessed January 27, 2012)

Grey, A. " Podcast 007 – 'Art, Love, Family, and Psychedelics' (Part 1)."
  Psychedelic Salon, Podcast Audio Program. 2005. Web,
  http://www.matrixmasters.net/salon/?p=22

Griffiths, R.R.. "Psilocybin as a Therapeutic Agent." *Neuroscene*, Podcast
  Audio Program. 2011. Http://neuroscene.com/?p=231.

-----. "Episode 69 -- Dr. Roland Griffiths :: Psilocybin and Mediation"." *The Secular Buddhist,* Podcast Audio Program. 2011. Http://www.thesecularbuddhist.com/episode_069.php.

Griffiths, R.R., K.A. MacLean, and M.W. Johnson. "Mystical Experiences Occasioned by the Hallucinogen Psilocybin Lead to Increases in the Personality Domain of Openness." *Journal of Psychopharmacology.* 0. no. 0 (2011): 1-9. http://jop.sagepub.com/content/early/2011/09/28/0269881111420188 (accessed November 23, 2011).

Griffiths, R.R., W.A. Richards, U.D. McCann, and R. Jesse. ""Psilocybin can occasion mystical-type experiences having substantial and sustained personal meaning and spiritual significance." *Psychopharmacology* 187, no. 3 (2006): 268-83

Griffiths, R.R., W.A. Richards, M.W. Johnson, U.D. McCann, and R. Jesse. ""Mystical-type experiences occasioned by psilocybin mediate the attribution of personal meaning and spiritual significance 14 months later." *Journal of Psychopharmacology* 22, no.6 (2008): 621-32

Institute of HeartMath. "HeartMath System FAQs, what is heart-based livinng [sic], personal coherence." http://www.heartmath.org/faqs/heartmath-system/heartmath-system-faqs.html (accessed September, 2012)

Jesso, J. "In Regards To A Crumbling Civilization" http://www.jameswjesso.com/in-regards-occupy-evolution-society/#more-478 (accessed January 10, 2012)

Jung C.G. *CW 9.1: Archetypes of the Collected Unconscious,* 2nd ed. Princeton, Nj: Princeton University Press, 1969

--------. "Psychology and religion", in *CW 11: Psychology and Religion: East and West.* New York: Pantheon Books, Inc., 1938

Lipton, B.H. *The Biology Of Belief: Unleashing The Power of Consciousness, Matter and Miracles.* Carlsbad Ca.: Hay House, 2008

Lucas, G. "Star Wars: Episode V - The Empire Strikes Back." 20th Century Fox Video. 2006. DVD

McKenna, T. *Food Of The Gods.* New York: Bantam Books, 1992.

----------. *True Hallucinations.* New York: HarperCollins, 1994.

Munn, H. "The Mushroom Of Language." In *Hallucinogens and Shamanism*, edited by M.J. Harner. London: Oxford University Press, 1973

Multidisciplinary Association for Psychedelic Studies. "MDMD-Assited Psychotherapy." http://www.maps.org/research/mdma/ (Accessed January 13, 2012)

O'Neil, M.J. ed. *The Merck Index: An Encyclopedia of Chemicals, Drugs, and Biologicals,* 14 Ed. New Jersey: Merck, 2006

Pinchbeck, D. *Breaking Open The Head.* New York: Broadway Books, 2002

Psychometric-Success.com, "The 'Big 5' Aspects of Personality." Last Modified September, 2010. http://www.psychometric-success.com/personality-tests/personality-tests-big-5-aspects.htm (Access May 25, 2011)

Ram Dass, *Be Here Now.* New York:Three Rivers Press, 1971

--------"Ram Dass - Love Serve Remember." Posted December 12, 2010. Web Video, http://youtu.be/8WPcpb2GHR4.

Redfeild, J., M. Murphy and S. Timbers. *God and The Evolving Universe: The Next Step In Personal Evolution*. New York: Penguin Putnam Inc., 2002

Roosevelt, F. "First Inarguable Address", Speech given at the United States Capitol on March 4, 1933.

Schultes, R. E., and A. Hofmann. *Plants Of The Gods: Their Sacred Healing and Hallucinogenic Powers*. Rochester, Vt.: Inner Traditions,1992

Shroomery.org, "Shroomery- How many dried mushrooms would I have to eat to die from an overdose of psilocybin?" Last modified October, 2006. http://www.shroomery.org/9122/How-many-dried-mushrooms-would-I-have-to-eat-to-die-from-an-overdose-of-psilocybin. (Accessed November 18, 2012)

----. "Shroomery – Psilocybin Awareness" Last Modified April, 2004 http://www.shroomery.org/6231/Psilocybin-awareness. (Accessed November 18, 2012)

Slater, L."How Psychedelic Drugs Can Help Patients Face Death - NYTimes.com." *The New York Times*, April 20, 2012. http://www.nytimes.com/2012/04/22/magazine/how-psychedelic-drugs-can-help-patients-face-death.html?pagewanted=all&_r=0 (accessed September, 2012).

Strassman, R. *DMT: The Spirit Molecule*. Rochester, Vt.: Park Street Press, 2001

Teeguarden, R. *The Ancient Wisdom of the Chinese Tonic Herbs*, New York, Ny.: Warner Books, Inc, 1998

TheCanadianDaily.ca. "Toronto destroys free community garden." Last Modified April, 2013. http://www.thecanadiandaily.ca/2012/10/03/city-of-toronto-destroys-free-community-food-garden-replaces-it-with-useless-grass/ (Accessed April 17, 2013)

Trungpa, C. *Shambhala: The Sacred Path of The Warrior*. Boston, Ma.: Shambhala Publications Inc., 1984

Vitatis, D. "SurThrival in the 21st Centaury." Seminar, from *The Light Cellar*, Calgary, Ab, June 3, 2011

Wasson, R. G., ""Seeking the magic mushroom: a New York banker goes to Mexico's mountains to participate in the age-old rituals of Indians who chew strange growths that produce visions." *LIFE*, June 1957.

Weil, A. "Cannabis Rx: Cutting Through the Misinformation." *Huffington Post*, September 12, 2010. http://www.huffingtonpost.com/andrew-weil-md/can-cannabis-treat-cancer_b_701005.html (accessed October 7, 2011).

Whitby, M. "LSD: The Beyond Within." British Broadcasting Company. 1986. VHS

Thanks for being awesome.

Check out more at:
http://www.jameswjesso.com
and
http://www.decomposingtheshadow.com

Made in the USA
Charleston, SC
15 April 2016